Life Hacks

(līf, hăks) noun.

Keith Bradford

Adams Media

New York London Toronto Sydney New Delhi

Adams Media
An Imprint of Simon & Schuster, Inc.
57 Littlefield Street
Avon, Massachusetts 02322

For information about special discounts for bulk purchases, please contact Simon & Schuster Special Sales at 1-866-506-1949 or business@simonandschuster.com.

The Simon & Schuster Speakers Bureau can bring authors to your live event. For more information or to book an event contact the Simon & Schuster Speakers Bureau at 1-866-248-3049 or visit our website at www.simonspeakers.com.

Interior illustrations by Kathy Konkle

Manufactured in the United States of America

20 19 18 17

Library of Congress Cataloging-in-Publication Data has been applied for.

ISBN 978-1-4405-8285-1
ISBN 978-1-4405-8286-8 (ebook)

Contents

Introduction

Congratulations! You've just opened the most helpful book on the face of the planet. Give yourself a big pat on the back because your life is about to change for the better. You'll now be able to get free food on your birthday, catch a liar in the act, unclog drains, stop mosquito bites from itching, charge your phone faster, and even survive a zombie apocalypse!

Life hacks have been around since the dawn of time, but they've just never had a title attached to them—until now. I still remember the first life hack I ever used. When I was a kid my grandma taught me an old trick that cured my hiccups within seconds. I was amazed! Well, I was mostly just happy to get back to playing soccer so quickly. But to this day, any time I get the hiccups, I still use her trick and poof, they're gone.

I started to realize that my grandma wasn't the only person that had secret tricks like this up their sleeve. Everyone seemed to have their own kind of tip or shortcut they used to hack their way through life. But imagine you could take everyone's tips, tricks, and shortcuts and put them all in one place; how great would that be? Oh wait, that's right, that's the book you're holding right in front of you!

Each of these life hacks entries have been pulled from various sources around the Internet as well as from user submissions from my blog 1000LifeHacks.com. Along with these are a ton more of my favorites that I've saved specifically for this book. They're all broken down into ten categories from technology to cures and solutions, so you can decide which aspect of your life you'd like to improve upon and start from there. It doesn't need to be read in chronological order either; you can literally flip to any page and start improving your life right now!

CHAPTER 1

Technology

1

Running low on battery? Put your phone on airplane mode and it'll charge much faster.

2

Want to download a YouTube video? Just add "ss" to the URL between "www." and "YouTube."

3

Need to test a printer? Print the Google homepage. It has all the colors you need to run a proper test, and will use almost no ink.

4

Get the Wi-Fi password to almost anywhere by checking the comments section on Foursquare.

5

If you mess up recording a voicemail, press "#" to re-record it.

6

Accidentally close a tab in your Internet browser? Press "Ctrl + Shift + T" to reopen it.

7

Out of "AA" batteries? You can use a "AAA" battery and fill the gap on the positive side with a small ball of tinfoil.

8

iPhone pictures will be of better quality if you take the picture and then zoom in on the saved version rather than zooming in while taking the picture.

9

Keep your charger from bending or breaking by sliding it into the spring from an old pen.

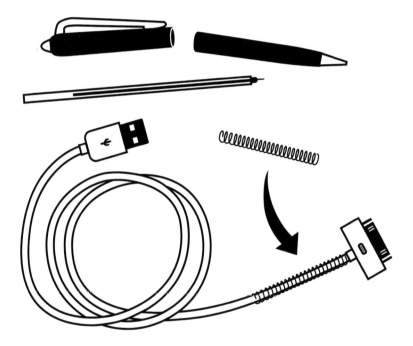

10
To listen to a song on YouTube on repeat, without having to keep pressing replay at the end, add "repeat" between "www.Youtube" and ".com."

11
Storing batteries in the freezer can double their lifespan.

12
Dropped your phone in water? Put it in a bag of rice. The rice will absorb the water and can potentially save your phone from death.

13

If an image is burned into your plasma TV screen, turn on static for the entire day. The image will fade away.

14

If you accidentally erased something you just typed on your iPhone, you can undo the action by simply shaking the phone.

15

When using Hulu, refresh the page at every ad-break. You'll only have to watch a thirty-second ad instead of a longer one.

16

If you have a computer that blocks sites like YouTube, Google Chrome's incognito mode will let you access them.

17

To resize a photo for Instagram, tilt your phone sideways and take a screenshot of it. It'll fit perfectly without affecting the quality.

18

Putting your phone on airplane mode will stop ads while playing games.

19

If you pause a YouTube video and type
"1980" you will have to fight off missiles to
protect your video.

20

Swipe left or right on the iPhone calculator
to delete the last digit, so you don't have to
start all over.

21

You can watch an awesome visualizer by
hitting "Command + T" while a song is
playing in iTunes.

10 Google Search Hacks

22 You can use Google search as a timer by typing in "set timer for" followed by the amount of minutes or hours you'd like Google to start counting down from.

23 Do you remember everything in your search term except for one word? Use an asterisk (*) in its place and Google search will fill in the blank for you.

24 Rather than sift through your local airport's website, simply type in the airline and flight number into Google search to get all the important information you need.

25 Turn the Google search page into pirate slang by typing in "Google pirate" and clicking the "I'm feeling lucky" button. "Settings" will now be referred to as "Me likes an' dislikes."

26 Want search results from one specific website? Type in your search term followed by "site:" and then the site you want the results from.

27 Don't bother getting out your calculator—you can simply type what you want converted like "20 euros to dollars" or "8 meters to feet" right into Google for an instant answer.

28 You can narrow your search to specific date ranges by typing in your search term and using ".." between the dates you want. For example, if you were searching for popular music during the mid-to-late 2000s, you could type in "Best albums 2004..2010."

29 Want to play Pac-Man? Go straight into the game by typing "Google Pac-Man" and clicking the "I'm feeling lucky" button.

30 Having something shipped to you? Don't bother going to a confusing shipping website! Simply type your package number into Google to take you straight to the tracking page.

31 Instantly translate between any language by typing in "translate" then your search term, followed by the language you want it translated to.

32

When sharing headphones with friends, turn on the mono audio feature, so that your phone splits the sound equally.

33

Want to save on your phone bill? Gmail offers free calling to anywhere in the United States as long as you have Internet and a microphone.

34

If you're in an area where you should have cell phone service but don't, put your phone on airplane mode and then switch back. This will cause your phone to register and find all the towers in your vicinity.

35

Tie a small knot around your left ear bud so you can easily tell them apart.

36

If you want to access Pandora, Hulu, or Netflix outside the United States, download the Chrome or Firefox extension called Media Hint.

37

Your headphones can be used as microphones if you plug them into the mic jack on your computer. This is helpful when recording lectures.

38

Go to *www.youtube.com/disco* and enter in an artist's name. YouTube will auto arrange an awesome playlist based on uploads of that artist.

39

Before you throw away a Post-it note, run it
between the keys on your keyboard to collect
dust, crumbs, and other things that might
get trapped in there.

40

You can go on NameChk.com to see every website where your username has been used.

41

Did your phone freeze? Plug it into a charger to free it up again.

42

Open an incognito tab in your browser and sign into Pandora to get unlimited skips for free.

43

Forget slow double clicks! Press "F2" on a PC and "Enter/Return" on a Mac to immediately rename a file.

44

Don't want the person you're calling to know
that it's you? Dial "*67" before the number
and he/she won't have a clue.

45

An iPad charger will charge your iPhone
much faster.

46

The Chromoji extension for Google Chrome
allows you to see emojis when you're on your
computer.

47

You can press "1," "2," "3," etc. to jump 10%,
20%, 30% into the video you're watching on
YouTube.

48

When letting someone use your iPhone to call someone, use Siri from the lock screen. They can call, but they can't look at your texts and photos.

49

Make an autocorrect shortcut on your iPhone or iPad to easily enter your e-mail address.

50

If you play YouTube videos through Safari on your iPhone, you can still listen to them with your screen turned off.

51

Can't afford Microsoft Word? Get OpenOffice; it's the same thing except it's free and has a lot more features.

52

If your camera ever gets stolen, go to StolenCameraFinder.com. You can upload an old photo from your camera and it will show you if someone has been posting images with the same serial number on the Internet.

53

If you lost an Android phone in your house and it's on vibrate, you can find it by logging in to Android Device Manager online and clicking ring.

54

To move frame by frame on a YouTube video, pause it and then use J or L to go backward or forward.

55

Ever wonder why phone cords are so short? Using your phone while it's charging can damage the battery.

56

Drop a battery from six inches off the ground. If it bounces once and falls over it's still good. If it bounces around more than that, it's dead or on its way out.

57

ProTuber is a free YouTube app on the iPhone that allows you to multitask while playing a video.

58

Hold down Alt and click on any Google image to have it automatically saved to your computer.

59

A quick and easy
iPhone speaker
using a toilet
paper roll.

60

When streaming Netflix on a computer, if the stream quality is sub-par, press "Control + Alt (Opt) + Shift + S" in order to change the buffering rates. Changing it to 3000 will give you HD video.

61

If you don't like a song on Pandora you can press the dislike button to automatically skip it and not use any of your skips.

62

If YouTube is forcing you to sign in, delete everything after the last "v=" and then change "v=" to "v/".

63

Confused by a Wikipedia article? Click "Simple English" on the left list of languages and it'll whisk you to a simplified version.

64

Cleaning out your Windows computer? Search "size:gigantic" and it'll display all the files on your computer greater than 128mb.

65

Tired of getting bombarded with spam? Keep two e-mail accounts with different passwords, so that one of these can be used exclusively for registering online accounts. This will prevent a ton of spam from hitting your inbox and your main account from being hacked.

66

Before going to a suspicious site, Google "safebrowsing:(website)" to see a ninety-day history of malware attempts on its visitors.

67

If your phone battery is really low and you need it for later, don't turn it off. Instead, put it on airplane mode. Turning it off and on will actually waste more battery than keeping it on airplane mode.

68

You can search "(month)(year)" in Wikipedia to give you all the major world news for that month.

10 Sites You Should Bookmark Right Now!

69 On Supercook.com you can enter what ingredients you have readily available and it will tell you what meals you can make as well as how you can make them.

70 10MinuteMail.com gives you a fake e-mail address so you don't have to use your own personal e-mail address when signing up for things.

71 Have a song stuck in your head but can't think of the name? Midomi.com will find it based on what you sing or hum into your computer or phone.

72 On AccountKiller.com you can instantly remove all of your personal data from websites you don't want having it.

73 Want to learn how to speed-read? Spreeder.com is a free website designed to improve your reading speed and comprehension.

74 Don't have a ruler? iRuler.net gives you an actual-sized virtual ruler.

75 Want to know if the file you downloaded contains a virus? Upload the file to Jotti.org and they'll tell you if it's safe to open.

76 At PrintWhatYouLike.com you can make your own printer-friendly version of a website. Print only the essentials, and reformat the page to print exactly what you want.

77 CopyPasteCharacter.com allows you to copy and paste symbols and special characters like copyright symbols, arrows, foreign currency, accented letters, and many more.

78 You can send any size file online for free at PipeBytes.com without uploading to a third party server.

79

Put glow-in-the-dark paint on your phone charger, so you'll never fumble in the dark for it again.

80

There's an app called Type n Walk which lets you see what's ahead of you while texting and walking.

81

Turning the flash off on your cell phone camera can extend your battery life even when you're not actually using the camera!

82

Tired of the tiny YouTube player when using a 20+-inch monitor? Simply hold "Ctrl" and scroll out (or "Ctrl + minus key") to increase the player size.

83

Want to download a YouTube video as an mp3?
Put "listento" after the "www." in the URL.

84

Instead of hitting backspace multiple times
to correct misspelled words, erase the whole
word by pressing "Ctrl + backspace."

85

Instead of using the "Ctrl + Alt + Del"
function to go to the task manager in
Windows, press "Ctrl + Shift + Esc" to open it
up right away.

86

Use bread clips to label your power cords so
that you can easily tell them apart.

87

Want to make sure you wake up in the morning? The Snooze app for iPhone will donate to charity each time you hit the snooze button.

88

Forgot your computer password? Boot up in safe mode (F8 during startup), log in as the administrator, and then change your password.

89

If you want to take an Instagram photo and save it to your phone without posting it, switch your phone to airplane mode.

90

The Along the Way app will give you any cool attraction you can see along the way of any road trip.

91

To make YouTube videos load faster, right click on the video, hit Settings, and move the "local storage" scroll bar all the way to the right.

92

When installing software always use the custom installation option. This will show you exactly what you're downloading and prevent you from installing unwanted toolbars and software.

93

When you copy something from the Internet use "Ctrl + Shift + V" to paste it. This will prevent the text from formatting.

94

In your e-mail inbox, search for
"unsubscribe" to find all of the newsletters
you never bothered to unsubscribe from.

95

Need to remember something in the morning?
Send yourself a text before you go to bed,
but don't open it until the next day.

96

You can use the volume + button on your
iPhone ear buds to take a photo.

97

By charging your laptop battery only up to 80% instead of 100%, you can greatly extend the usable lifespan of the battery.

98

Can't read the text on a website? Press "Control +" to zoom in on a PC and "Command +" to zoom in on a Mac.

99

When writing an e-mail, make sure the last thing you do is put in the recipient's e-mail. This will help you avoid sending an unfinished e-mail.

100

Turn any cord into a coil cord by wrapping
it tightly around a pen and blow-drying it
for two to three minutes.

101

When moving or redecorating, take a picture
of the back of your TV or tech equipment to
easily remember how everything hooks up.

102

CMD.fm is a site that allows you to listen
to any genre of music with unlimited skips
for free.

103

Change the lock screen on your phone to a picture of your name and contact information like an e-mail address or home number. That way if you lose your phone, the person who finds it can easily see whose phone it is and how to get the phone back to you.

104

When watching a DVD, press Stop, Stop, Play, and Skip to skip the ads and go straight to the movie.

105

To skip a YouTube ad, just change "youtube" to "youtubeskip" in the URL of any video.

106

If you want to ignore someone, simply add them into your phone contact list as "ignore" and make the ringtone of that contact silent.

107

When signing up for a website, don't answer the security questions honestly. You'll actually protect your account and identity more if you always use the same wrong answers.

108

iOS 7 has a built-in horizontal and vertical leveler. Open the compass and swipe to the left to access it.

109

The FastCustomer app will never make you wait on hold again. It calls the company for you, waits on hold, and then calls you when an actual human is on the line.

110

The program DeTune will transfer all of the songs from an iPod or iPhone onto your computer.

111

You can enter a show you like on Televisor.com and it will recommend new shows to watch and where to find them online.

112

Fix a scratched CD or DVD by rubbing a peeled banana on it and then buffing it out with the outside of the peel.

113

View blocked sites by clicking the "cached" button beside the link on a Google search.

114

Try the Sleep Cycle app for the iPhone. This bio-alarm clock measures your sleep cycle and wakes you up at the lightest point in your sleep, meaning no more groggy mornings!

CHAPTER 2

Food and Drink

115

Have leftover coffee from the morning? Use it to make coffee ice cubes, which will cool down your coffee without diluting it.

116

Run your bacon under cold water before cooking it. Doing so will reduce shrinkage by up to 50%.

117

If your water starts foaming over the pot when you're boiling it, pour in a couple tablespoons of olive oil. It'll stop overflowing almost instantly.

118

Poke a fork through the creamy part of an Oreo, so that you can dip the whole Oreo in milk without getting your fingers wet.

119

When making tacos, put the cheese on first.
It will melt and form a protective layer that
keeps the taco shell from breaking apart.

120

Any citrus fruit like an orange, clementine,
or grapefruit becomes easier to peel when
you gently press and roll it on the table
before peeling.

121

Put pancake mix in an empty ketchup bottle
for a clean, no-mess experience.

122

An old CD spindle makes for the perfect bagel
holder. They are great for packing lunches.

123

If you peel a banana from the bottom, you won't have to pick the little "stringy things" off of it.

124

When making hard-boiled eggs, throw one teaspoon of baking soda into the water. The shell will come off without a problem once the egg is cooked.

125

Insert a drinking straw into a ketchup bottle to make it flow out faster.

126

Wrap a soft tortilla around a crunchy one. It'll hold everything much better and you can put beans and cheese between them for the ultimate taco experience.

10 Foods That Get Rid of an Upset Stomach

137

Reheat leftover pizza on a frying pan. It'll keep the crust from getting soft.

138

Cut your pack of bacon in half for easier baking, cleaner storage, and a better size for making sandwiches.

139
The unspoken restaurant language.

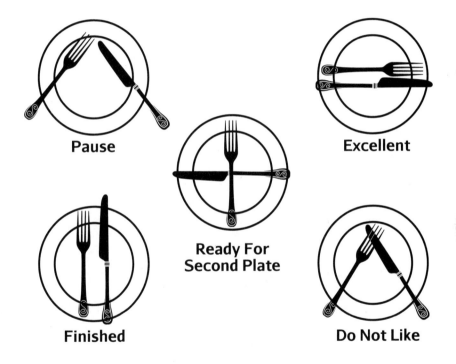

Pause

Ready For
Second Plate

Excellent

Finished

Do Not Like

140

When it comes to staying awake, apples are actually more powerful than caffeine.

141

You can ripen your avocados more quickly by placing them in a brown bag with bananas for 24 hours.

142

Trying to cut sugar out of your diet? Freeze bananas. They're much sweeter when frozen, making for a great, tasty treat.

143

When you want to put a two-liter bottle of soda away, shake it up a little bit first. It will stay fizzy for weeks.

144

Soak Oreos in half-and-half and lay them on wax paper in the freezer. In an hour, each one will be a delicious mini ice cream sandwich.

145

Ice cream too frozen to scoop? Don't microwave it; simply run the spoon under hot water.

146

Ketchup can be used to clean copper pots and pans. The acid in ketchup removes tarnish and makes copper shine.

147

Hate when your Hot Pockets explode in the microwave? Stab it with a fork before you put it in.

148

Wrap the stems of your bananas in plastic wrap to prevent them from browning so quickly.

149

The less you eat sweets, the less you will crave them. It's really that simple.

150

Cottage cheese and sour cream will last twice as long if you turn the container upside down. This forms a vacuum seal and prevents bacteria from getting in.

151

To tell if an egg is fully cooked or raw, just spin it. If the egg wobbles, it's still raw. If it spins easily, it's fully cooked.

152

Tired of your takeout food getting cold by the time you get home? Put it in your passenger seat and turn on the seat warmer.

153

Microwaving lemons and other fruits for fifteen seconds can double the amount of juice you get from them.

154

Turn your spoon upside down when pouring milk into a bowl of cereal to prevent splashing.

155

You can use the lid of a yogurt or applesauce container when you don't have a spoon handy. You can also twist one of its ends to use as a handle.

156

Buy bananas in various degrees of ripeness, so that you'll have a ripe one to eat every day.

157

Did your soda get shaken up? Tap the sides, not the top, to prevent bubble buildup and soda explosion.

158

Cauliflower dipped in barbecue sauce tastes almost the same as chicken nuggets—and it's way healthier.

159

Use frozen grapes to cool down wine without having to water it down.

160

Put three different Kool-Aid ice cubes in a cup; add Sprite and a shot of vodka. The flavor of the drink will change as the ice melts.

161

Microwave your pizza with a small amount of water in a glass to keep the crust from getting chewy.

162

Popcorn actually pops better when it's stored in cold places like the refrigerator.

163

How to make simple yet delicious Nutella Cookies: Mix 1 cup Nutella, 1 whole egg, and 1 cup flour together in a bowl. Bake for 6–8 minutes at 350 degrees.

Tired of jelly soaking through your peanut butter and jelly sandwiches? Spread the peanut butter on both sides of the bread and put the jelly in the middle.

Did your tortilla chips get a little stale? Toss them in the oven for 10 minutes at 375 degrees. They'll come out just like new!

166

Have you ever made a S'moreo? Simply twist open an Oreo and place melted chocolate and a roasted marshmallow in between the cookies.

167

An empty Pringles can makes for a perfect container for your raw spaghetti.

168

Put sprinkles in the bottom of the ice cream cone to prevent leaks.

169

You can order Starbucks drinks at "kid's temperature." The drink will be much cooler and you'll never burn your tongue again!

170

Need to cook a whole bunch of hot dogs at once? Toss them all in a Crock-Pot.

171

Trouble with chopsticks? It's perfectly acceptable to eat sushi with your hands since that's the way it was originally done in Japan.

172

To keep potatoes from budding, toss an apple in the bag.

173

Watermelon can help relieve stress and anxiety, keep you energized, and boost your metabolism.

174

Want to stop crying when chopping onions? Just chew gum.

175

Making cookies and don't have eggs? Sure, you could ask the neighbor, but half a banana (per egg) works as a great substitute.

176

Want to make a drink cold really fast? Wrap it in a wet paper towel and put it in the freezer for two minutes.

177

Want a quick and easy dessert topping? Crush up Oreo cookies and put them in a salt grinder.

178

You can unroll the rim of ketchup cups to increase their capacity.

179

Turn bread upside down while cutting
it. This will save you from getting those
annoying squished slices that nobody wants.

180

Use condiment bottles filled with icing for
an easy way to decorate cookies and cakes.

181

Buying ice cream? Press on the top of the
container. If it's solid, it's been properly
stored. If it can be pushed down, it's been
thawed and refrozen.

182

Want to cut a watermelon open without a knife? Take a quarter, make a small incision at the center of the watermelon, and karate chop it in half. No joke, it actually works!

183

Make stale cookies soft again by putting them in a plastic bag with a piece of bread. Leave it overnight and they'll be almost good as new.

184

Boiling water before freezing it will give you crystal clear ice.

185

Push a straw through the middle of a strawberry to easily remove the stem.

186

Open your bag of chips from the bottom since most of the flavoring has sunk there.

187

Shake a can of mixed nuts before you eat them. The larger ones will always rise to the top.

188

Hate having bread ends? Turn the outward sides inwards to make a sandwich. This is perfect for little kids since they'll never know the difference.

189

Microwaving Nutella and milk in a mug will give you the best hot chocolate ever!

10 Fast Food Secret Menu Items

190   Dairy Queen's Frozen Hot Chocolate: A hot chocolate blended with ice to give it a frosty crunch.

191   McDonald's Big Mac Poutine: McDonald's classic golden fries topped with their famous Big Mac sauce.

192   Wendy's Grand Slam: Also known as the Meat Cube, this burger has a total of four patties.

193   White Castle's Seasoned Fries: You can get your fries with additional seasoning free of charge.

194   Starbucks Nutella Misto: Order a Caffè Misto with a shot of chocolate and hazelnut topped with caramel drizzle.

195   Popeyes Naked Sandwiches: At any Popeyes, you have the option to get your sandwich "naked," which means no breading on your meat.

196   Long John Silver's Side of Crumbs: A free box of batter parts that have fallen off the fish or chicken. It's a great topping for salads.

197   Dunkin' Donuts Turbo Hot Coffee: A coffee with an extra shot of espresso in it.

198   Burger King's Frings: Can't decide between fries and onion rings? Order the Frings and they'll give you half and half.

199   McDonald's Monster Mac: A Big Mac made with eight meat patties.

200

Onions and garlic are both foods that accelerate your hair growth.

201

Overcooked your bacon while making breakfast? Crumble it and add it to your scrambled eggs.

202

Before frying, sprinkle a little salt in your pan. This will help keep the oil from splattering.

203

Eating grapes improves the brain's ability to process new information and thus enhances your intelligence.

204

When heating leftovers, space out a circle in the middle of the food. The empty space will help your food heat up much more evenly.

205

Avocados boost serotonin levels. Eating them is a good way to improve your mood and relieve depression.

206

How to avoid rotten eggs.

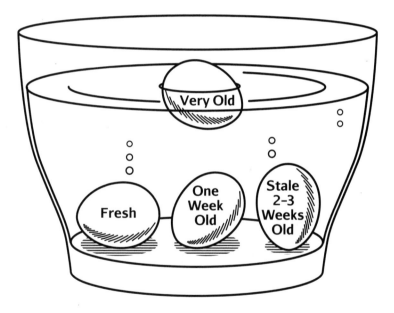

207

Stuff marshmallows before you roast them. The possibilities are endless, but chocolate chips, peanut butter cups, and strawberries are always great fillings.

208

To make BLTs, or any toasted sandwich, place two slices of bread in a single toaster slot. This way, the bread gets toasty on the outside, but stays soft and chewy on the inside.

209

Want to save time when cooking a dozen eggs? Put them in a muffin tin, set the oven to 350 degrees, and bake them for 15–20 minutes. They'll come out the perfect size for an English muffin breakfast sandwich.

210

Tired of messy cake cutting? Run your knife under hot water, dry it off, and then cut your cake. Works like a charm. You may need to re-heat it a few times if you're cutting a whole cake.

211

Drinking a cold glass of water in the morning will wake you up faster than a cup of coffee.

212

Need more kitchen space? Slip a cutting board over an open drawer, so that you have another shelf to store utensils, oven mitts, or other small kitchen knickknacks.

213

Bake your cookies in a muffin tin. They'll stay soft and fluffy, and won't spread out as thin as they normally would.

10 Stress-Relieving Foods

214 Bananas

215 Pasta

216 Almonds

217 Grapes

218 Green tea

219 Oatmeal

220 Chocolate

221 Watermelon

222 Orange juice

223 Tuna

224

Microwave a Nature Valley bar for thirty seconds to prevent crumbs when you eat it.

225

Oysters, lean meat, seafood, and whole grains are all foods that have been proven to boost sex drive.

You can add two eggs and half a cup of oil to turn any cake mix into cookie dough.

It's completely safe to eat the stickers that are on fruit. Even the glue used to put them on is food grade.

Has your champagne lost its bubbly-ness? Drop a raisin in and watch the bubbles magically return.

229

Kiwi fruit contains lutein, an antioxidant than can actually help improve eyesight.

230

Use waxed, unflavored dental floss to
cleanly slice a cake.

231

Put melted chocolate and strawberries in
an ice cube tray and freeze for several
hours. These decadent cubes will make for a
refreshing summer treat.

232

Pour pancake batter over strips of bacon to
make the best pancakes ever.
You won't regret it!

If you're a vegetarian, don't try and make your pets vegetarians, too. It can kill them.

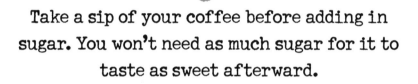

Take a sip of your coffee before adding in sugar. You won't need as much sugar for it to taste as sweet afterward.

Can't get that garlic smell off your hands? Rub them on stainless steel for 30 seconds before washing them.

236

Peanut shells are edible; you don't actually have to take them off to eat the peanut.

237

Friend got the blues? Make them a package of Cookie Dough Oreos by replacing the cream filling of an Oreo with cookie dough. They will instantly feel better.

238

Place a piece of wax paper on top of your ice cream to prevent freezer burn.

239

Before cutting up a pineapple, place it upside down in the freezer for thirty minutes. Since all the sugar sinks to the bottom of the fruit, this disperses it.

CHAPTER 3

Health and Fitness

240

When you feel the urge to drink or smoke, go for a run, do twenty sit-ups, or some other activity that will get you moving. You'll soon start to associate quitting the habit with being fit.

241

Gatorade and Powerade are only healthy when used during a workout, and watered down. Otherwise, it's mostly extra sugar and empty calories.

242

When you're thirsty and limited water is available, rinse your mouth for thirty seconds before swallowing. Most of your "thirst" comes from a dry mouth.

Exhale when your left foot hits the ground
to avoid cramps while running.

Drinking two cups of water before meals can
make you lose an average of four and a half
more pounds in twelve weeks.

Recipe for relaxation: Exhale completely,
inhale for four seconds, hold your breath for
seven seconds, and exhale for eight seconds.

246

Listening to music while working out can boost
your running and lifting ability by 15%.

247

Eliminate stress and headaches by resting in this position for five minutes.

Eating a small amount of chocolate in the morning can actually help your body burn calories and lose weight throughout the day.

A cup of coffee before a workout speeds up the fat burning process.

Honey, when mixed with vinegar and water, can remove worms and other parasites in your body.

Getting the right amount of sleep is crucial for your immune system. Sleeping for more than nine hours at a time can actually damage it!

Skipping meals can cause your body to go
into a fat-storing starvation mode, making
it harder to burn calories.

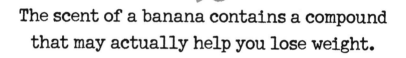

The scent of a banana contains a compound
that may actually help you lose weight.

Because of their high lycopene content,
eating tomatoes may help prevent sunburns.

Feeling depressed? Drink water; you may be
chronically dehydrated.

5 Simple Weight Loss Tips

256 Drink more water.

257 Adjust your portion sizes.

258 Lower your sugar intake.

259 Limit carbs to one time per day.

260 No fast food.

Eating celery is technically exercise.
When you eat celery, you burn more calories
digesting it than you consume.

Drinking sixteen ounces of water will
increase your metabolism by up to 30%.

263

Want to lose weight? Don't eat anything four hours before you go to bed. It really makes a huge difference.

264

Cold showers may help relieve depression and will keep your skin and hair healthy.

265

Eating breakfast in the morning makes it ten times easier to burn calories throughout the day. It also makes you less likely to get acne.

266

The more organized you are, the less likely you are to develop Alzheimer's disease.

267

You can use a tube sock as a simple workout armband.

268

Pineapple juice is five times more effective than cough syrup. It also prevents colds and the flu.

269

If you want good running form, try to run as quietly as possible. You'll be able to run faster and longer.

270

The cells in your body react to everything that your mind says. Negativity actually brings down your immune system.

271

Drinking five cups of green tea in a day can help you lose weight around your belly.

10 Reasons You Should Drink More Water

272 It increases energy and relieves fatigue.

273 It helps your body lose weight.

274 It reduces your risk of getting kidney stones or a UTI (urinary tract infection).

275 It improves your skin's complexion.

276 It helps digest your food, preventing constipation.

277 It boosts your immune system.

278 It acts as a natural headache remedy.

279 It prevents cramps and sprains by keeping your joints lubricated.

280 It puts you in a good mood.

281 It saves you money! Water is free. In fact, fast food restaurants legally have to give you water for free if you ask.

Yawning actually cools down your brain,
which helps get rid of stress.

283

Smiling for sixty seconds, even when you're
in a bad mood, will immediately improve
your mood. Using these muscles is enough to
trigger the happy chemicals in your brain.

Always exercise on Monday. This sets the
psychological pattern for the rest of the week.

285

Need some motivation to go to the gym?
GymPact is an app that will pay you for
working out and punishes you for missing
out on days.

286

When you find yourself looking in the fridge out of boredom, drink the biggest glass of water you can find. You'll be too full to want food.

287

Drinking chocolate milk has been proven to help relieve muscle soreness after a workout.

288

Stretch for five minutes before going to bed. Your muscles will be more relaxed and it'll be easier to find a comfortable position to sleep in.

289

You can "rewire" your brain to be happy
by simply recalling three things you're
grateful for every day for twenty-one days.
Try it!

290

If you're going for a run, the jog.fm app
will select a music playlist for you based
on your pace.

291

Rub deodorant between your thighs to keep
them from chafing when you wear shorts.
You're welcome!

292

Moderate alcohol drinkers gain less weight
over time than people who don't drink at all.

293

Don't wet your toothbrush after you put toothpaste on it. Water reduces some of the healthy benefits of using toothpaste.

294

You can burn up to 180 calories while watching a horror movie.

295

Eating plenty of unsalted sunflower seeds is a great home remedy for reducing your cholesterol level.

296

Want to lose weight? Eat more spicy food. Spicy foods trick your taste buds into being more satisfied with smaller amounts of food.

297

Drinking fruit juice doesn't even come close to the benefits of eating fruit. Fruit juice often contains more sugar and a lot less fiber.

298

Laughing for fifteen minutes has the same health benefits as getting two extra hours of sleep.

299

Trying to eat less? Use a smaller plate. It tricks your mind into thinking there's more food, and also limits what you can pile onto your plate.

300

Too much stress literally causes the human brain to freeze and shut down temporarily.

301

Memorizing songs is extremely healthy for your brain and will improve your mental capacity.

302

Eat an orange before working out. Not only does it keep you hydrated, but it also prevents your muscles from getting sore.

303

Losing one night of sleep will impair reasoning and brain function for four days.

304

When you're stressed, try eating 1 cup of low-fat yogurt or 2 tablespoons of mixed nuts. The amino acids in them will help calm you down.

10 Activities to Get Rid of Anxiety

305 On a piece of paper, write down a list of your skills.

306 Read that list two or three times a day.

307 Do some yoga poses and meditate.

308 Exercise to increase your endorphins.

309 Pinpoint areas of stress in your life and figure out how to change them.

310 Visit an alternative-healing practitioner.

311 Spend time with people you enjoy being around.

312 Set a daily routine.

313 Stop avoiding things out of fear.

314 Practice affirmations.

315

Eating watermelon can help reduce acne breakouts and keep skin healthy.

316

Lip biting triggers a rush of chemicals to the brain, which reduces anxiety, stress, and instantly boosts your mood.

317

Daytime naps help to improve your memory and cut the risk of heart disease.

318

Never be embarrassed to cry. Crying releases stress hormones and is scientifically proven to relieve stress.

319

By simply owning a cat, your risk of heart attack decreases by 30%.

320

By thinking one positive thought every morning, you can psychologically trick yourself into being a happier person.

321

Learning to play a musical instrument or learning another language can actually slow down the aging process of the human brain.

322

Working out before bed makes your muscles burn more calories throughout your sleep cycle.

323

When you're feeling down or depressed,
do some cleaning. Straightening out the
physical aspects of your life can also bring
clarity to the mental ones.

324

If you're stressed, try running. Outside
of meditation, it's one of the best ways to
clear your mind.

325

The faster you eat, the more weight you gain.
A study showed that a fast eater gained more
than four pounds over eight years, while a
slow eater gained only one and a half pounds.

326

Mustard and toothpaste will help ease the pain of minor burns.

327

Doing 7,000 jumping jacks burns enough calories to lose about one pound. Spread that over a week and you'll lose an extra pound every week.

328

If you fall asleep within five minutes of going to bed, it's an indication that you're extremely sleep deprived.

329

In order to lose a pound of fat, you'll have to run for more than 3 hours. If you run for 27 minutes every day, you can lose a pound in a week.

330

Get stung by a bee? Apply a cut onion to the area. This will help break down the chemicals responsible for inflammation and discomfort.

331

Not only is exercising good for your health, but it also has been known to increase your brain power by 10%.

Make your playlists as long as you plan to exercise. This will make you focus more on your workout and keep you from constantly looking at the clock.

333

Don't want to miss leg day? Use the rowing machine. It works legs, arms, and abs.

CHAPTER 4

Cures and Solutions

334

Mosquito bite? Apply a hot spoon onto the spot. The heat will destroy the reaction and the itching will stop almost instantly.

335

If someone presses all of the buttons on an elevator, you can avoid stopping on each floor by pressing each button again twice.

336

Candles will burn longer and drip less if they are placed in the freezer for a few hours before using.

337

Have a splinter? Pour a small amount of white glue on the area. Let it dry and peel it off. The splinter should come right out.

338

Don't want to be embarrassed when buying something? Buy an inexpensive birthday card with it.

339

Got a headache that just won't go away? Take a lime, cut it in half, and rub it on your forehead. The throbbing should go away.

340

If you want to get rid of bad breath, brushing your teeth is important, but what's more important is brushing your tongue.

341

Wrinkly shirt? Throw it in the dryer with a few ice cubes for five minutes.

342

You can heal paper cuts and immediately stop the pain by rubbing ChapStick on the wounded area.

343

Getting nauseous from reading in the car? Tilt your head side to side and it'll go away.

344

Use a clothespin while hammering. You'll
never bang your thumb again!

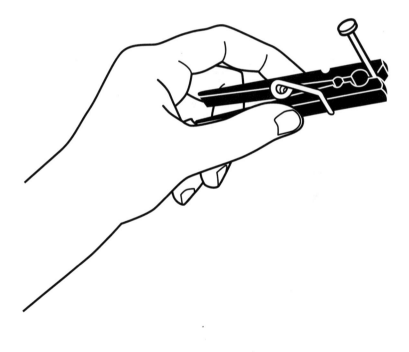

345

Pee shy? Start multiplying random numbers in your head. The same part of the brain controls both tasks and will help you get started.

346

If you have sensitive ears, put Vaseline on earrings before putting them on. This should prevent irritation.

347

To stop a Popsicle from dripping on your hands, pierce a muffin cup liner with the stick so it catches the drizzle before it hits your hands.

348

Drinking a tablespoon of apple cider vinegar will relieve allergy and asthma symptoms.

349

Standard blackboard chalk will remove grease stains. Simply rub the stain with the chalk and toss it in the wash like normal.

350

Not sure if you have bad breath? Lick your wrist and smell it. This is what your breath smells like to others.

351

When your dog gets out, don't chase it; lie down and pretend you're hurt. They'll always come back to see if you're okay.

352

Runny or stuffy nose? Push your tongue against the top of your mouth and push a finger between your eyebrows. Hold it for about twenty seconds. Your nose should clear.

353

Gum stuck to your clothes? Boil vinegar and pour it over the gum. Use a brush to wipe off. The gum will come off instantly!

If you have painful gas, lie on your back and lift your knees to your chest. You'll fart it right out.

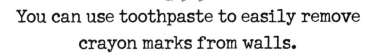

You can use toothpaste to easily remove crayon marks from walls.

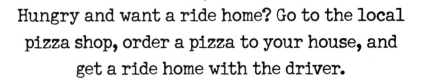

Hungry and want a ride home? Go to the local pizza shop, order a pizza to your house, and get a ride home with the driver.

To cure a sore throat, add a teaspoon of honey to JELL-O mix and heat it up. The gelatin will coat and soothe your throat.

358

Get something in your eye? Fill up a bowl big enough for your face with water and open your eyes in it. The irritating object should come right out.

359

Need some change? Put your cash into a vending machine and hit the coin return button without ordering anything.

360

Want to use your phone in the rain or on the beach? Put it in a Ziploc bag. The touch screen still works under the plastic and you'll still be able to hear the person on the other line.

Turn your steering wheel 180 degrees before parking in the sun. This way, you won't burn your hands when you start driving.

Shoes smell bad? Put them in the freezer overnight. It will kill the bacteria and get rid of the stink.

If you ever want to stop a sneeze from coming, simply press your tongue against the roof of your mouth and it'll vanish.

364

Accidentally get deodorant on your shirt?
Rub a dryer sheet over the area to
remove it completely.

365

Soak a cotton ball in vinegar and put it on a
bruise to make it disappear.

366

To prevent loud noises and backsplash in
a public restroom, put toilet paper in the
toilet beforehand.

##

Instead of scraping ice off your car, try spraying it with a mixture of $^2/_3$ cup vinegar and $^1/_3$ cup water. The ice will melt right off.

368

Flattened pillow? Put it in the sun for thirty minutes. The sun will absorb any moisture caught in the pillow and plump it up.

##

Are your thoughts keeping you awake at night? Try writing them all down. This clears your head and makes it easier to fall asleep.

370

Rubbing alcohol will remove pen marks and stains from pretty much anything.

371

The best way to cure hiccups is to actually try to hiccup.

372

Shoes too small? Put on three pairs of socks, put the shoes on, and blow dry for ten minutes. They'll fit perfectly now!

373

Put toothpaste on a pimple and it will disappear overnight.

374

Exhale as much air as possible to suppress laughter at inappropriate times.

375

Wrap rubber bands around the ends of coat hangers to prevent dresses from slipping off.

376

If your cat loves to sit in front of the computer, flip the top of a box upside down and set it to the side. Boxes are like magnets for cats.

377

Accidentally text the wrong person?
Immediately put your phone on airplane mode
and once it fails to deliver, delete the message.

378

Guys: Flex any muscle for sixty seconds to
get rid of an unwanted erection.

379

Placing an envelope in the fridge for an
hour will unseal it. Good tip to know if you
forget to include something in a package.

380

Have a headache? Eating ten to twelve
almonds is the equivalent of taking two
aspirins for a migraine headache.

If you ever clog the toilet in a public restroom and there's no plunger, pour some liquid hand soap in. Let it sit for 5 minutes and flush again. This could save you someday.

To remove gum from your hair, dip the strands into a small bowl of Coke for a few minutes. You should be able to wipe the gum off with a comb.

383

If a shirt or sweater has static cling, put a safety pin in it. The static will instantly go away.

384

How to know where to stop when parking in your garage.

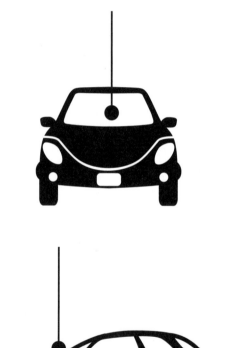

Make homemade ice packs by adding one part rubbing alcohol to three parts water in a Ziploc bag. It will get cold but not hard, so you can easily wrap it around sore body parts.

If you stand up too fast and start to black out, tighten your abs as hard as you can.

Hate getting those squeaky, wobbly, or bumpy carts at the grocery store? Try grabbing one from the parking lot before you enter the store. People usually ditch the bad ones inside, and it also gives you a chance to test it out before you start shopping.

388

It may sound crazy, but white wine will actually take out a red wine stain.

389

Drinking two glasses of Gatorade can relieve headache pain almost immediately, without the unpleasant side effects caused by traditional pain relievers.

390

Put clear nail polish onto the outer threads of a button to keep it from unraveling or popping off your jacket or sweater.

391

Hate the feeling of putting cold eye drops in? Run the bottle under hot water for a few seconds. You'll barely feel them.

392

Have an itchy mosquito bite? Put some Wite-Out on it. The correction fluid will stop the itch within seconds!

393

When a bag of chips is stuck in a vending machine, don't buy the same bag again to unjam it; buy something right above it.

394

When you are at the pool or beach, set your flip-flops face-down. This prevents them from being scalding hot from the sun when you're ready to leave.

395

Pimple too painful to pop? Put it under hot water for a few seconds. This softens it and makes it easier to pop.

396

If you're at a hotel and run out of chargers, the TV usually has a USB plug-in. No computer charger? Hotels usually have a bunch in their lost and found.

397

If you're feeling nervous, start chewing gum. Your brain will reason that you're not in danger because you wouldn't be eating if you were.

398

Put a stocking over a vacuum cleaner to find tiny lost items like earrings.

399

Remove gross, unpleasant odors in smelly shoes or gym bags by placing dry tea bags in them and leaving them there overnight.

10 Tricks to Help You Quit Smoking

400 Go to a sauna three days in a row. You'll sweat out the nicotine and it'll be easier to quit.

401 Drink a lot of water and chew fennel seeds. This will help flush toxins out of your system. The fennel seeds will keep your mouth active when cravings arise.

402 Buy the cheapest, most disgusting cigarettes you can and smoke those. It will help your willpower.

403 Lick a little salt with the tip of your tongue whenever you feel the urge to smoke. This is said to break the habit within a month.

404 Keep active. When you feel the urge to smoke, go for a run to keep your mind off of smoking. You'll also start to connect living a healthier lifestyle to quitting.

405 Download the QuitNow! app. It keeps track of health improvements, cigarettes not smoked, and money saved while you're quitting.

406 Reward yourself. Along with the health benefits, quitting smoking saves you a lot of money, so treat yourself every once in a while to give you extra motivation.

407 Don't quit cold turkey. About 95% of people that quit without therapy or medication end up relapsing.

408 Use smoking as a stress reliever? Try finding a new way to manage stress like regular massages, listening to relaxing music, doing yoga, or practicing tai chi.

409 Clean your house. Once you've quit, make sure to completely clean out your house. Throw out your lighters, matches, empty packs of smokes, and anything that smells like smoke.

410

Get rid of nighttime coughs by putting Vicks VapoRub on your feet and then placing socks over them. Your cough will stop within minutes.

411

Spam texts bothering you? Forward them to 7726 and your carrier will reply asking for the number it came from to help stop spam.

412

Putting Tums on a painful mouth ulcer will cause it to go away in a matter of hours.

413

Eat something really spicy? Eating
a teaspoon of sugar will completely
neutralize the heat sensation.

414

If you wet your fingertips and the head of
the nail clippers, the nail clippings won't
fly off when you trim your nails.

415

Putting apple cider vinegar on moles, warts,
and skin tags will remove them.

416

Smelly jeans? Put them in a Ziploc bag and freeze overnight. The same technique works for shoes.

417

The gel from an Advil liquid gel will cure a pimple almost instantly.

418

If you accidentally over-salt a dish while cooking, drop a peeled potato into the mix. The potato will absorb the excess salt.

419

To instantly untangle headphones, pick a point about halfway along the wire and shake it.

420

Squeezing a lemon or lime into your shampoo
will stop frizzy hair.

421

Acne Scar Remedy: Mix a teaspoon of nutmeg
and a tablespoon of honey into a paste. Apply
for thirty minutes and rinse. Repeat daily,
if needed.

422

Want to cool down your body temperature?
Run your wrist under cold water for at least
five minutes. It'll cool your blood down.

Tired of getting between zero and seven Tic Tacs when you shake the container? Avoid that by letting the mint gently glide into the tiny crevice in the lid.

424

Having trouble sleeping? Look at photos of other people sleeping. This triggers a response in your brain that actually makes you feel more tired.

425

Stuffy nose? Leave a sliced onion near where you sleep and let it sit for the night. Your nose will be clear by the time you wake up.

426

Putting vodka on your face tightens your pores and reduces the chances of acne breakouts.

427

Bad sunburn? Aloe lotion is good, but aloe ice cubes are better!

428

Immediately applying Mineral Ice Pain Relieving Gel to a burn will prevent blistering.

429

Take note of your body's position in the morning. This is probably your most comfortable sleeping posture, so posing this way before bed can help you get to sleep more quickly.

430

Got stains on your sneakers? Scrub them with nail-polish remover and the stains will come right out.

431

Get rid of fruit flies by filling a bowl with apple cider vinegar and a bit of soap. The vinegar will attract them and the soap will kill them.

432

If you're experiencing insomnia, drink a glass of raw lemon juice or a spoonful of honey before sleeping. This will drastically improve your sleep.

433

Remove a splinter by applying a paste of baking soda and water for several minutes. The splinter should pop out of the skin.

434

If you're out of shaving cream, use olive oil. It works just as well, if not better.

435

As soon as you have brain freeze, push your tongue against the roof of your mouth. It will relieve the pain instantly.

Have a sore throat? Try eating a piece of cucumber. It cools down your throat and stops that itchy feeling.

Need to get rid of the hiccups? Hold your breath and swallow three times.

Put a sticker with a fake PIN number on your debit card. That way, if you lose it and someone tries to use it more than three times, the machine will eat the card.

439

Get rid of rust by rubbing it with aluminum foil soaked in vinegar.

440

Zipper won't stay up? Flip it to the down position. Most people don't know that this "locks" the zipper.

441

Can't brush after a meal? Gargle salt water. You'll be amazed at all the gunk that comes out!

442

Singing releases a large amount of endorphins in your brain and can make you feel better almost instantly.

443

Shoes smell funky? Use dryer sheets as an incredibly effective shoe deodorizer.

444

Adding vodka to your shampoo can strengthen your hair, prevent dry scalp, and stop dandruff.

445

Cornstarch will untangle all kinds of knots. Rub some into shoelaces, chains, and string to easily loosen them up.

446

Tape a toy snake to the top of your car when you park and you'll never have another bird poop on it again!

447

According to a study, smelling rubbing alcohol can relieve nausea almost instantly.

448

Need to get those annoying stickers off a product? Spray it with a liquid that contains alcohol, like perfume. The alcohol eats at the glue adhesive, allowing for easy removal.

449

Need to remember an item in the morning? Put a picture of it as the background for your phone.

450

Hate insects? Take vitamin B complex
during the summer to ward off mosquitos
and biting flies.

451

Eat something too spicy? Drink milk. It will
neutralize the spicy taste in your mouth.

452

If you're coughing uncontrollably, raise
your hands above your head and it will stop.

453

Having trouble sleeping? Blink fast for a
minute. Tired eyes help you to fall asleep.

454

People are more likely to return a lost wallet
if they find a baby picture inside of it.

455

Use toothpaste to clear up hazy car
headlights—always works like a charm!

456

If you drop an earring, ring, or small screw,
simply turn off the lights and look for it
with a flashlight. It should light right up
once you scan over it.

457

If you're a smoker and can't or don't want to quit, drink more black tea. It helps prevent the lung damage caused by smoking.

458

Get something in your eye? Using your fingertips, hold your eyelashes and pull down your eyelid. Blink rapidly several times to get rid of the foreign object.

459

Applying crushed aspirin to a wart and covering it with duct tape for several hours will make it disappear.

460

Did you know that it's beneficial to lick small cuts? A variety of compounds in human saliva can speed up healing.

461

The 20-20-20 Rule: Looking at something 20 feet away for 20 seconds every 20 minutes is a method proven to stop eye strain and headaches.

462

Holding a banana peel over a bruise for ten to thirty minutes will almost completely remove its color.

463

Suffering from acne? The problem could be
your pillowcase. Sleeping on a fresh one
every night will usually solve the problem.

464

Mix 3 mint leaves, ½ cucumber, ½ lemon,
and 1 cup filtered water for the perfect
headache remedy.

465

Have a stomachache? Lie on your left side
and rub your stomach in clockwise circles.
It actually helps!

466

Don't burn yourself with those hard-to-reach candles. Use a stick of raw spaghetti to light the wick.

467

No bug repellent? Put dryer sheets in your shoes and in your pockets. It will help keep mosquitoes away.

468

Inhale through your mouth, swallow saliva twice, and slowly exhale through your nose for a 100% effective hiccup cure!

469

Ever have that thing in the back of your throat that makes you want to gag and cough it out? Scratch your ear and it'll go away.

470

Reading a book before bed makes your eyes tired. As a result, your brain is tricked into feeling tired and falling asleep is much easier.

471

Toothpaste removes ink from your clothes. Apply it to a stain, let it dry, and then wash your clothes.

472

The most effective cough syrup that exists is honey.

473

Have a headache? Submerge your feet and hands in hot water and put a bag of frozen peas on the back of your head. The heat on your extremities pulls the blood from your head, relieving your head pains.

474

Chugging one glass of grape juice can relieve migraine headaches almost instantly.

475

Can't tell if a woman is big or pregnant? Ask her if she has kids. She'll mention if she's pregnant.

476

Having trouble falling asleep? Count backwards from ninety-nine. Chances are, you'll fall asleep before you even get to fifty.

477

Drinking a tablespoon of apple cider vinegar in the morning can help fight arthritis pain throughout the day.

478

Clogged drain? Unclog it with 1 cup of baking soda mixed with 1 cup of white vinegar.

479

Showering with cooler water can help stop dandruff.

480

Gum on your shoe? Spray it with some WD-40
and it'll come right off.

481

Babies keep crying when you hold them? Try
raising your eyebrows instead of furrowing
them. Babies are observant of faces, so
they'll be less likely to cry.

482

Blow some air in when filling up water
balloons. This will cause it to pop when it
hits someone instead of just bouncing off.

483

If you lose something, take a picture of your room, put it on Facebook, and have your friends play "I Spy."

484

Don't have a coin to flip? Look at the time. If the minutes are even, it's heads, and if they're odd, it's tails.

485

When you're in pain, cursing releases enkephalin, which raises your pain tolerance, causing you to hurt less.

486

Do you have blue hands from your new jeans? Wash them with a tablespoon of salt to set the dye.

487

Zipper keeps falling down? Attach the zipper to a key ring and put it around your pants button.

488

Get rid of your motion sickness by sucking on a lemon or eating olives.

489

Have a pounding migraine headache?
Try eating spinach instead of popping a
pill. Magnesium is used in the ER to treat
migraine attacks, and spinach contains
loads of magnesium as well as riboflavin.

490

Sleepy but don't want to be? Hold your
breath as long as you can and then breathe
out slowly. This will perk you right up!

491

When you feel like you're about to yawn,
touch the roof of your mouth with your
tongue to prevent it.

CHAPTER 5

Money Savers

492

If you bought something on Amazon and the price goes down within thirty days, you can e-mail them and they will send you the difference.

493

When ordering coffee, ask for a medium in a large cup. The baristas will have to estimate the amount in a medium, so you usually get a lot more coffee than what you paid for.

494

When grocery shopping, the cheapest items will be on the top and bottom shelves, not at eye level.

495

On the bottom of every Krispy Kreme receipt is a plea to fill out a survey. You get a free doughnut for doing the survey. When you get your doughnut, you get another receipt, with another survey. Free doughnuts for life!

496

You can get $100 off any vacation package from Delta Airlines if you book that trip during your birthday month.

497

Restaurants are required to give you free water. A good tip to know if you're running in the heat.

498

LOZO.com will give you coupons for each item on your shopping list.

499

For frequent Starbucks customers: Buy and use a membership card. It only takes five transactions to get to the green level, and then coffee and tea refills are free.

500

When buying from a vending machine, insert your lowest value coin first. If the machine isn't working, you won't lose that much money.

501

Target will price match Amazon. If you find something cheap on Amazon, buy it at Target instead and you won't have to wait for it to be shipped to you.

502

Every November 7th is "Bring Your Own Cup Day" at 7-Eleven.

503

Always ask for a discount when buying jewelry. You'll usually be able to get a good one.

504

In automatic car washes, the basic wash is just as good as the deluxe one. Those three-color soaps in the deluxe are just gimmicks, a ploy designed to get you to pay more for the same thing. All the actual cleaning of the car is done with regular soaps, which are included in every package.

505

You can get a free cup of Dippin' Dots during your birthday month. Just sign up for their e-mail and they'll send you a coupon!

506

Buying a gym membership? Most times, your health insurance company will completely reimburse the cost for you.

507

When shopping online, search for promo codes on Google before making a purchase. You can usually find a variety of discounts from free shipping to 25% off.

508

Never buy shoes again! Payless will replace any shoes you buy from them regardless of how long you've had them or what you've put them through.

509

Never go to the grocery store hungry. You'll end up buying several things you don't actually need.

510

If you have a gift card with less than $10 on it, the business is legally required to give you the rest of your balance in cash if you ask.

511

You can get a free 20-ounce Dr Pepper, 7UP, Sunkist, Canada Dry, or A&W at 7-Eleven just by downloading their app!

512

Buying a car? Buy it at the end of the month. Salespeople usually have quotas to meet and will be more likely to cut you a deal.

10 Best Places to Get Free Wi-Fi

513 McDonald's

514 Starbucks

515 Panera Bread

516 The Apple Store

517 Your local museum

518 Staples

519 The Courtyard Marriott

520 Barnes & Noble

521 Office Depot

522 Your local library

523

Download the Apple free app of the week even if you don't need it. You can delete it and re-download it whenever you want for free!

524

Want to save some cash during the holidays? Send candy boxes that are less than 13 ounces. You don't have to repackage it; just slap on a stamp and address and toss it in the mail.

525

Put a binder clip at the end of your
toothpaste tube to get every last bit.

526

When a price at Costco ends in $.97, it's their clearance price and that's the lowest it will ever go.

527

With the promo code "9ANY" you can get any pizza you want at Pizza Hut for $9 when you order online.

528

Too broke to travel? WWOOF is an organization that allows you to travel the world, with food and accommodations covered, in exchange for volunteer work.

529

Most car washes have a rain check policy where if it rains within 48 hours of your last visit, you can get your car washed again for free.

530

Don't buy new ink cartridges for your printer. Take the old ones to Costco and get them filled for only $10.

531

Renting a movie from Redbox? Put two movies in your cart, remove one, and then go to checkout. An offer will come up for a discount on a second movie.

532

On Halloween, any kid can get a free scary face Halloween pancake at IHOP.

533

If a Duracell battery leaks and destroys one of your devices, the company will replace the device if it's sent to them with the defective batteries still in place.

534

Don't pay to learn a new language! You can learn Spanish, French, Italian, German, and Portuguese for free on Duolingo.com.

535

If you cancel your Hulu Plus trial before the seven days are up, they'll give you the next month for free.

When going over 40 mph, it is more economical to have the windows up and AC on. While driving under 40 mph, the opposite is true.

While flying, sign up for the free thirty-minute trial of on-board Wi-Fi. Delete the cookies when trial ends and start a new trial.

If you have an ".edu" e-mail address, you can get a free Amazon Prime account. This lets you watch many TV shows and movies via Amazon.

539

Each 5 mph you drive over 60 mph is like paying an additional 10 cents a gallon for gas.

540

On Viberly.com, you can get a free subscription to Netflix or Spotify simply by putting a sticker on your laptop!

541

Getting premium gas for a car is said to make almost no difference in performance.

542

Ordering a six-piece box of McNuggets from McDonald's? It's actually cheaper if you order two four-piece boxes instead.

543

If you want to get a new laptop, phone, or other electronic device, get it in October. You can usually get up to 40% off most electronics.

544

Extra bacon and extra cheese is free
of charge with the order of a Bacon
Cheeseburger at Five Guys.

545

On SNESFUN.com, you can play almost every
single Nintendo game for free.

546

Want a magazine subscription but don't want
to pay full price? Local libraries usually
don't take out those little cards that list
cheaper subscriptions.

547

If you ask a pickle stand employee at
Disneyland how their day is, they'll give you
a free pickle.

548

When buying something from Craigslist, use a fake e-mail address to lowball the seller by a lot. Then, using your regular e-mail address, offer a reasonable but still lower price. People will usually go for the second offer.

549

Starbucks offers an even smaller size than tall called a short. It's cheaper and a much healthier size.

550

Two Domino's medium two-topping pizzas online are cheaper than buying one from the store.

551

At Chipotle, there's no limit to the number of tortillas you can order on the side.

10 Places to Get Free Stuff on Your Birthday

552 IHOP: Free stack of pancakes.

553 Medieval Times: Free admission to the show when you sign up for the King's Court Club.

554 Dunkin' Donuts: Free cup of coffee.

555 Sephora: Free mystery makeup gift bag.

556 Cinemark Theatres: Free tub of popcorn.

557 Baskin-Robbins: Free scoop of ice cream.

558 Missouri: One free lottery ticket.

559 Waffle House: They offer a variety of free birthday meals.

560 Starbucks: Free drink if you're a rewards member (which is also free to sign up for).

561 Kmart: Free $5 to spend in their store.

562

Get your first Redbox movie rental for free!
Just type in "dvdonme" when it asks for a
promo code.

563

FuelMyRoute.com will tell you the lowest
possible gas prices along your route.

564

When taking a cab somewhere unfamiliar to
you, put your destination in your phone's
GPS. This way, it will be impossible for the
driver to scam you.

565

You can extend the length of a free trial by
pushing back the date on your computer.

566

Several studies have shown that gasoline expands and contracts by 1% for every 15 degrees the temperature changes. It tends to be cooler in the morning, which means the gas is more contracted and you're getting more volume per dollar than when it's warmer in the afternoon.

567

If the taxi driver asks if you're "from around here," lie and say yes. Sometimes they drive farther (driving up the price) for tourists.

568

Grocery stores stack their products by sell-by date, which means the oldest food is in the front. Make sure to always grab food from the back.

7 Things You Should Know Before Booking a Flight

569   Use your browser's incognito tab or delete your history every time you go online to check flight rates. The prices actually go up when you visit a site multiple times.

570   Six to eight weeks before you want to book your flight is the cheapest time to buy.

571   The cheapest days to buy tickets on are Tuesday and Wednesday.

572   The cheapest days to fly on are Tuesday, Wednesday, and Saturday.

573   Sunday is usually the most expensive day to fly.

574   Prices change up to three times per day.

575   Discount ticket sales are usually offered at the beginning of the week.

576

Ask your local pizza place if they have any orders that people didn't pick up. They will usually let you have them at a discount price.

577

If you buy a bag of Starbucks coffee and return the bag when it's empty, they will give you a free 12-ounce cup of coffee.

578

The first Friday of June is National Doughnut Day. You can get a free donut at Krispy Kreme, no purchase necessary!

579

By peeing in the shower, you can save about 1,157 gallons of water a year.

580

You can buy gift cards at up to 35% off their value from CardCash.com.

581

Close with your neighbors? Share your Wi-Fi and split the bill.

582

How to easily calculate a 20% tip: Take the total cost of your bill and move the decimal one place to the left. Double that number to get your 20% tip.

583

To save money when you shop, don't touch anything. Touching an item makes you more likely to buy it.

The Cinemark app will give you free popcorn vouchers and other rewards if you can keep your phone silent and screen dimmed during the movie.

585

If you send Mickey and Minnie Mouse an invitation to your wedding, they'll send you back an autographed photo and a "just married" button. Here is the address:

Mickey & Minnie
The Walt Disney Company
500 South Buena Vista Street
Burbank, CA 91521
USA

CHAPTER 6

Life Tips

Fold your receipt around the gift card after you use it so that you always know your balance.

Have a good twenty-minute workout in the morning. Then you won't feel bad about lounging for the rest of the day.

If you ever go to a zoo, wear the same colors as the employees do. The animals will come right up to you.

Need to tell a believable lie? Make sure to include an embarrassing detail about yourself. Nobody will doubt a story that makes you look dumb.

590

Hanging out with someone that's new to your group of friends? Call your friends by their names, so that the new person has a chance to memorize them.

591

Have a tough decision to make? Flip a coin. Not to decide for you, but you'll realize what you really want when it's in the air.

592

Put your home number in your cell phone's contact list under "Owner." That way, if someone finds it, they can easily contact you.

593

Never ask someone how his or her job search is going. It's going terribly until they tell you they got a new job.

594

Take pictures of friends holding items you've
lent them with your phone, so you remember
down the road who borrowed what.

595

Thinking about sex will temporarily relieve
the urge to pee in the case of an emergency.

596

Buy a house or apartment near a hospital.
During a blackout, your electricity will
always be restored before everyone else's.

597

Make sure you buy a fire extinguisher before
you need a fire extinguisher. Same thing goes
for a plunger.

598

Never base your life decisions on advice from people who don't have to deal with the results of your decision.

599

If your car is about to get towed, get in it. Tow trucks are forced to stop to avoid kidnapping charges.

600

Don't ever leave a sports game early. The most historical games were made in the final seconds.

601

When doing your nails, use Elmer's glue around your nail, let it dry, and then go crazy with the nail polish. Peel off the glue to reveal perfectly manicured nails.

602

Want to watch a movie with a girl? Ask her what her favorite movie is and say you haven't seen it. She'll usually say, "We should watch it."

603

While driving, move your seat as far back as you can while still being able to touch your pedals. This will help prevent speeding.

604

Get invited to a wedding? Set the date as a recurring event in your calendar, so you can wish them a happy anniversary every year.

605

Learning from your mistakes is wise, but learning from the mistakes of others is quicker and easier.

606

If you ever need to stop and ask for directions, skip the gas station and find a pizza delivery place. They know their way around town way better.

607

If you need a stranger to take a photo of you, make sure it's someone you know you can outrun.

608

If you are buying headphones or speakers, test them out with "Bohemian Rhapsody." It has the complete set of highs and lows in instruments and vocals.

609

Make a password into a goal of yours so you're constantly reminded of it.

610

Listening to music literally changes your brain's perception of time and reduces the amount of time you think you're waiting. This is why they always have music playing in waiting rooms.

611

Never keep condoms in your wallet. After just a month in there, it has a 50% greater chance of breaking.

612

If you forget someone's name simply say, "Sorry, what was your name again?" They may look annoyed, but once they tell you their first name say, "No, I meant your last name."

613

When flying with a group of friends or family members, make sure to mix up your clothing between the suitcases. That way, if a bag gets lost or stolen, one person isn't completely screwed.

614

For the best sound in a movie theater, sit two-thirds of the way back and as close to the middle as possible. This is where audio engineers sit when they mix sound for movies.

615

Making a blanket fort? Use a fitted sheet instead of a normal blanket for a sturdier and more practical roof.

616

Use ketchup packets as ice packs. They're the perfect size for a kid's bumps and bruises and they stay soft enough to form around any body part.

617

Take a picture of yourself when your hair looks good. Show it to the barber the next time you get a haircut to ensure you get perfect hair every time!

618

Never say "sorry" to another driver after a car accident. It's an admission of guilt and could be used against you in court.

619

Never sleep naked. If there is some kind of emergency, it might be too late to put something on.

620

Try and eat at least five home-cooked meals a
week. A recent study shows that doing so makes
you 47% more likely to live an extra decade.

621

You can see if a certain pair of jeans will
fit without trying them on by placing the
waistline around your neck.

622

Keep a card with all your emergency contact
numbers and medical information on it in
your wallet. It could save your life someday.

623

Simply touching money has been proven to reduce physical and emotional pain.

624

The next time you stub your toe or get a cut, look away. The body oftentimes associates pain with sight.

625

Make friends with three people: a law student, a police officer, and a bartender.

626

At a restaurant, you'll never go wrong ordering the chef's favorite dish.

627

At Disney World, you can actually request a wake-up call from any Disney character you want!

628

When you get a call from a telemarketer, don't say anything and press "9" on your phone. This will automatically add your number to their "don't call" list.

629

Get caught doing something embarrassing in public? Just say you lost a bet.

630

If someone has to try and convince you it's not a pyramid scheme, it's a pyramid scheme.

631

If you wear a Yelp shirt to a restaurant,
you'll get the best service ever.

632

When buying something online, only read the
reviews that gave three stars. They're usually
the most honest about the pros and cons.

633

Never go shoe shopping late at night. Your
feet can get 5% to 10% larger at the end of the
day than in the morning.

634

Before you get a tattoo, think of what you
would have gotten five years ago. This may
change your mind.

635

The Two-Minute Rule: If you see something that needs doing and it can be completed within two minutes, do it immediately.

636

If you ever want to call a family meeting, just turn off the Wi-Fi router and wait in the room in which it's located. You'll round up the family in about ten minutes!

637

Buying something from Amazon? Buy it on Smile.Amazon.com since part of the proceeds goes to a charity of your choice.

638

Put things back where you first looked for them, not where you found them.

639

You can call 311 for non-emergency calls to the police.

640

Try applying your deodorant at night instead of in the morning. It'll be more effective and you'll sweat less the next day.

641

Slurping your food loudly at Japanese restaurants is actually seen as a positive gesture and indicates to the chef that you're enjoying the food.

642

If you ever have to park in a city at night, park in front of a bank. They're lit up and have cameras everywhere.

643

Not only is vodka good for Friday night fun,
but it can also be used as hair conditioner,
bug repellant, and to soothe jellyfish stings.

644

Don't know what to get someone for their
birthday? Have them make three guesses of
what you got them. You now have three ideas
on what to get them!

645

When you're at a restaurant, wash your
hands after ordering. The menu is generally
the dirtiest thing you can touch.

646

When filling up your car with gas, hold the
trigger halfway. You'll get more gas and less
air in the tank.

647

Going to the beach? Clear out an old lotion bottle and put your phone, money, and keys in it for safer keeping at the beach.

648

Make sure to clean your suitcases after staying in a hotel. Bed bugs often make the journey from the hotel room to your home via your suitcase.

649

Finding it hard to meet people? Go outside when it's raining with a huge umbrella and take your pick.

650

It's been proven that sleeping on your right side will help you fall asleep faster than sleeping on your left.

651

If you buy unnecessary things that are on sale, you're not saving money; you are still spending it.

652

If a job makes you pay money to work for them, it's a scam. Period.

653

"Rhythm," "zephyr," and "sphynx" are the three best possible hangman words.

654

Never use your favorite song as your alarm clock—you'll just end up hating it.

655

Never make the wrong turn on the freeway again: The alignment of the tabs on top of exit signs tells you whether the exit will be on the left or right.

Think of being with someone you love the moment before you get your picture taken. You'll end up with a natural smile every time!

When starting a game of "rock paper scissors" always start with paper. Most people start with rock just because it's the shape the hand easily forms.

658

Hang a picture of a tattoo you want somewhere you'll see it every day for a year. If you still want it after that, then it's worth getting.

Truck drivers are always communicating with
each other on the road. If you see one slow down
for no reason, there's probably a cop ahead.

Whenever you make a packing list for a trip,
make two copies. Use one to pack and the second
to make sure you bring everything back.

661

Learn to drive a stick. You'll be more
focused on the road, your car is less likely
to be stolen, and it's fun!

When you feel like you need something, but
you can't figure out what it is, it's water. It's
always water.

If you're walking in a bad area at night, call someone and stay on the line. If something happens, they can call the police.

How to get kids to behave on road trips: Bring a bag of candy. Anytime they misbehave, throw a piece of candy in the car trash. It may be kind of mean, but it works!

Take a picture of business cards people hand you, just in case you lose them.

On camera, wearing yellow makes you look bigger and wearing green makes you look smaller.

667

Microwave two big bowls at the same time
by elevating the second bowl with a mug or
another small, microwave-safe container.

Always go out in public dressed like you're
about to meet the love of your life.

Secretaries, tech support, and janitors are
the true power in an office. Make friends
with them and you'll be able to get anything
you need!

670

Golden spending rule: If you can't afford two
of it, you can't afford it.

671

If you're at a Japanese restaurant, never
rub your chopsticks together. It's a gesture
that's extremely offensive to the chef.

672

Never be embarrassed about farting; it helps reduce high blood pressure and is extremely beneficial to your health.

673

Want to make sure you always get fresh fries at McDonald's? Ask for them unsalted. They'll make a fresh batch, and they also offer salt packages at the condiment counter.

674

When on a date, the best way to judge a person's character is to see how they treat waiters and waitresses.

675

Instead of going to dinner and a movie, go to the movie first and then dinner. This way, you have something to talk about at dinner.

676

When you're thinking about buying something you don't necessarily need, imagine the item in one hand and the cash in the other. Which one would you take?

677

Tie a small piece of brightly colored fabric to your luggage. You'll be able to spot your bag at the airport in no time!

678

Try going twenty-four hours without complaining (not even once) and watch how your life starts changing.

679

Can't find someone to help you in an
electronics store? Stand by the biggest,
most expensive TV and look at the price tag.
Someone will be right over.

680

Don't let yourself be controlled by three
things: people, money, and past experiences.

681

Fall in love with someone's eyes. It's the one
thing that never changes.

682

If you're driving into a town and don't know what to do, call a hotel and say that you're staying there next week. They'll be more than happy to answer any questions that you ask.

683

The phrase "don't take this the wrong way" has a 0% success rate.

684

The date rape drug Rohypnol tastes very salty. If your drink suddenly has a salty taste, stop drinking it immediately.

685

Success is a state of mind. If you want success, start thinking of yourself as a success.

686

Learning an instrument can improve your IQ by up to seven points. Don't want to pay for lessons? JustinGuitar.com offers completely free guitar lessons.

687

If you're with Verizon, AT&T, T-Mobile, or Sprint, you can now text the police (911) in case of emergency.

688

Pay attention to how your boy/girlfriend treats their family. Eventually that's how they will treat you.

689

Getting married at age twenty-five or older significantly decreases risk of divorce by over 60%.

690

Feeling ugly? Go sit in Walmart for two hours. You will feel a lot better!

691

Take advantage of power outages. It's the best possible time to get a good look at the night sky.

692

Try to spend more money on experiences and less on things. You'll thank yourself later on in life.

693

To tell if you're dreaming or not, check a clock twice. If the time is drastically different from the first time you checked, you're definitely dreaming.

694

Never loan a friend more than you can afford to give away.

695

Good things come to those who wait, but greater things come to those who get off their ass and do anything they possibly can to make it happen.

696

When buying a romantic card, get two. Write the inscription from card A into card B and pretend you can write sweet things. Be sure to use with caution.

697

Always check your motorcycle helmet for spiders before driving down the highway.

698

If you have to put a beloved pet to sleep, find a vet who will make a house call. You'll feel better knowing that the animal's last hour won't be spent in a place it hates.

699

Saying "Boots 'N' Cats" quickly, repeatedly, and at varying tempos is the secret to beatboxing.

700

If you ever find a driver's license, you can put it in any mailbox as is and the postal service will return it to its owner.

701

Parents of seven- to sixteen-year-olds can make their children behave in public by threatening to sing loudly.

702

Wearing headphones do not make your farts silent. Please keep this in mind.

703

Make note of what someone does for you when you're sick. It's probably the same thing that comforts them the most when they don't feel well.

704

In a public bathroom, the stall that is the closest to the door is usually the cleanest because it's the least used.

705

Studies have shown that dancing has been known to improve relationships. It can strengthen the couple's bond and relieve emotional tension.

706

Always under-promise and over-deliver. Most people tend to do the opposite.

707

In order to be a good liar, you need to convince everyone that you are a bad liar.

708

If your car is ever overheating, don't keep driving it. Two minutes of overheating is enough to completely ruin your engine.

709

Never be afraid to spend a little extra on a new bed and shoes. If you're not in one, you're in the other.

CHAPTER 7

Survival

710

If you ever get trapped underwater in your car, use your car seat's headrest to break the window.

711

If you ever get kidnapped and they tie your hands together and put tape over your mouth, lick the tape. It will eventually fall off and you'll be able to yell for help.

712

If you get buried under snow by an avalanche, spit and saliva will follow gravity. Dig the opposite way.

713

If you're ever attacked by a swarm of wasps or bees, use hairspray to immobilize them.

714

If you're about to get hit by a car and can't jump sideways, jump up! It'll give you a better chance of surviving.

715

When you call 911, the first thing you should always say is your location. They immediately send police when they have an address.

716

Short on firewood? Make a Swedish Flame.
Make your cuts like you're slicing a cake.
Leave about six inches at the base. Throw
about half a cap of fuel oil in. It will burn
for two to three hours.

717

Not sure if you're in a bad neighborhood?
Look at store windows. Plate glass means
you're in a good one; plate glass with bars
means you should leave before dark; and if
you see plywood, leave immediately.

718

Any working cell phone, regardless of
whether it is in service or not, will call 911.

719

If you're on a road trip and can't pay for a
motel, park at Walmart and sleep in your car.
They won't kick you out!

720

Drinking helps fight against radioactive poisoning. The only survivors of Chernobyl were drunk at the time.

721

Want to take a nap on public transit but are scared of getting your bag stolen? Put your leg through the loop or handle. If someone does try to take it, you'll feel them tugging at it.

722

If you're swimming toward the shore and find yourself moving out, you're caught in a riptide. Swim parallel to the shore to escape it.

10 Tips for Your Next Camping Trip

723 Keep your toilet paper dry by putting it in an old CD spindle. It fits perfectly.

724 Tossing some sage into the campfire will keep you bug-free all night.

725 Use "joke candles" (the ones that can't get blown out) to light fires. This way, the wind won't affect the flame.

726 Put some glow-in-the-dark paint on your tent so you can easily navigate back to it at night.

727 Blow into an acorn cap with your two thumbs over it if you ever get lost in the woods. This will make a loud high pitch whistling sound for other hikers or campers to hear.

728 In order to get fewer burs, rub the laces of your hiking boots with paraffin before hitting the trail.

729 Use biodegradable marking tape to mark your hiking trail so that you never get lost.

730 Putting deodorant on an insect bite will stop the itch instantly.

731 Never get your matches wet. Store them in a small Tupperware container and glue a piece of sandpaper to the inside of the lid for a place to spark your matches on.

732 Never wear the Calvin Klein "Obsession" scent when camping. It has been known to attract cheetahs, tigers, and jaguars!

733

If you ever suspect that someone is
following your car, take four right turns.
It will form a circle, and if they're still
behind at that point, then they're definitely
following you.

734

If you ever get stuffed in a trunk,
disconnect the backlight wires. When a cop
pulls them over or you're at a red light, kick
the door so that people know you're there.

735

Out of candles? A crayon will burn for up to
thirty minutes!

736

Homemade Camping Lamp: Strap a headlamp to a gallon jug of water. Your tent will fill up with ambient light.

737

Falling air pressure causes pain in birds'
ears, so if birds are flying low to the
ground, it almost always means that a
thunderstorm is coming.

738

Sitting in the back of a plane makes you 40%
more likely to survive a crash.

739

When using a riding mower on a slope, mow
up and down, not sideways. About ninety-five
Americans are killed each year because of
not knowing this.

740

Need to give CPR? Compress their chest hard to the beat of "Stayin' Alive" by the Bee Gees. The tempo is the correct timing of compressions.

741

If you're ever attacked by a brown bear, play dead. If it's a black bear, punch it in the nose and it will run away.

742

When you see a halo around the sun or moon, get indoors immediately. This means a storm is coming.

743

If you're in for a long drive at night, listen to comedians. It's impossible to fall asleep while laughing.

744

To escape from a crocodile's jaws, push your thumbs into its eyeballs. It will let you go instantly.

745

If you get stuck in quicksand, raise your legs slowly and lie on your back. You can't sink in this position.

746

If you're ever homeless, spend whatever money you have on a twenty-four-hour gym membership. You'll not only have a place to go at night, but will also be able to use their showers to stay clean.

747

Don't put your feet up on a car's dashboard. Airbags go off like small bombs and can easily break both of your legs.

748

If you're outside in the woods and cut yourself, spider webs will not only seal the wound, but also make it heal much faster.

749

Find water in the wild by creating a solar still using a container, plastic sheet, and drinking tube.

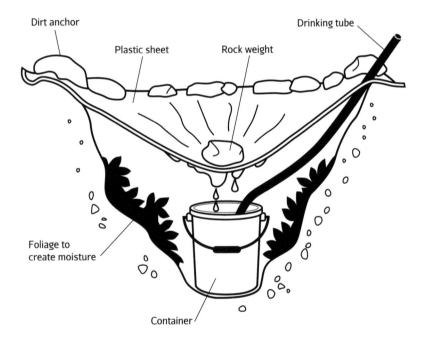

Dirt anchor

Drinking tube

Plastic sheet

Rock weight

Foliage to create moisture

Container

750

Doritos work great for kindling if
you can't find any.

751

If you ever get buried alive, take your shirt
off and tie it around your face and mouth to
keep from suffocating.

752

Find yourself without a source of fresh
water? Get a cup full of dirty water and
run a piece of cloth between that and an
empty cup. After a few minutes, you'll have
filtered, muck-free water. Remember to boil
it before drinking.

To heat your food without electricity or fire, cut the wide side of a small box, fold it outwards, and wrap it completely with aluminum foil. Place your food inside and wait for the sun to warm it up. Hello, solar-charged grilled cheese!

754

Start a cooking fire easily by filling an egg carton with charcoal and lighting each corner.

Need to open a tuna can, but don't have a can opener? Just rub the top of the can on concrete for a minute and then squeeze the sides in. The top will pop open.

756

No compass? Get a small sliver of metal like a needle and rub it against your clothing several times. Place it on a leaf and float it in some water. The needle will always point north.

757

Need a makeshift oil lamp? Fill an empty soda can halfway with olive oil. Twist an old cloth and stick it in the can so that only the top pokes out. Light and enjoy the light for hours.

758

Bees can't see you if you aren't moving.

759

Always carry pepper spray when in bear-
infested woods. Spraying it can stop them from
charging at you from up to thirty feet away.

760

Get your change stuck in a vending machine?
Don't mess with it. Vending machines kill
more people per year than sharks do!

761

You can make rainwater drinkable by boiling
it or using about eight drops of bleach per
gallon of water.

10 Tips for Surviving a Zombie Apocalypse

762 Always have a solid pair of running shoes on. You never know when you're going to have to run next.

763 Go to Costco. These warehouse stores have large cement walls, an endless supply of food, and you have to have a membership card to get in.

764 Everyone knows a zombie's weakness is its head. Make sure you have a good head smasher like a bat or some sort of a club.

765 Only use guns in desperate situations. Noise is what attracts zombies; guns are like dinner bells to them!

766 Wear a bandanna over your face. Thousands of zombies roaming the earth isn't going to smell pleasant. Plus, the humans that do survive probably aren't going to be putting hygiene at the top of their list.

767 Wearing thick clothing can quite possibly save you from being bitten and "turning."

768 Get inside safe, large walls. Like in *The Walking Dead*, a prison can be a great place to start.

769 Always have some energy or granola bars available. Food is going to be hard to find, and chances are, your local grocery stores are going to get raided. Plus, you never know when you're going to need a burst of energy!

770 Never go to the hospital. Although they have medical supplies that will help your endeavor, they are usually where the outbreaks start and, thus, are usually the most infested places.

771 Avoid grouping with children, pregnant women, and fat people. Instead, try to befriend doctors, athletes, and scientists. This will greatly improve your chance of survival.

772

Outside during a lightning storm? Avoid open fields, elevated mountaintops, and watery areas. Try to isolate yourself between rocks or in caves and never lie flat on the ground.

773

If you ever come across a pack of wolves in the wild, the worst thing you can possibly do is look them in the eyes.

774

If you're ever in a building during an earthquake, the national standard is to drop, cover your head or neck, and hold even for a few minutes after the rumbling has stopped.

775

Out of toilet paper? Use dead, dry leaves supported by one green leaf in the middle. This will ensure you'll never use poison ivy by mistake.

776

Whenever you're going on a camping trip, always make sure that someone who's not on the trip knows where you're going and when you'll be back.

777

Homemade Wasp Catcher: Cut off the top of a soda bottle, flip it over, and place it back onto rest of the bottle except upside down. Pour some sugar water into it and hang it in the area where you've had wasp problems.

778

Mix Mountain Dew, baking soda, and peroxide
to make a homemade lantern.

779

Walking in a scary area at night? Download
a police scanner app for your phone and
listen to it on full volume.

CHAPTER 8

Party Hacks

780

Mixing alcohol with Diet Coke will get you drunker than if you mix it with regular Coke.

781

Four words to get free alcohol at a party: I've never been drunk.

782

Going to a bar? Start by giving the bartender a $20 tip. You'll get amazing service for the rest of the night.

783

How to open a beer with another beer.

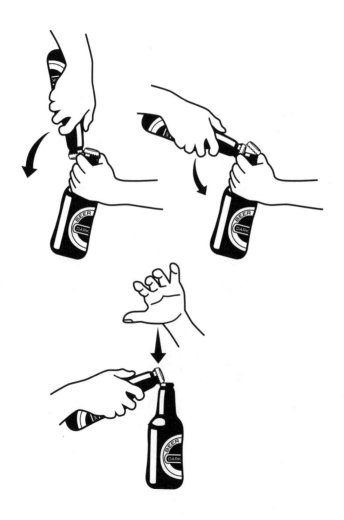

784

Need a ride home on New Year's Eve? Call AAA insurance. They will pick anyone up and drive them home free of charge.

785

Always hold your drink in your left hand at parties. That way, your right hand won't be cold or wet when you shake someone's hand.

786

Feel the urge to vomit? You can stop yourself by eating a mint or chewing minty gum.

10 Tips for Hosting a Summer BBQ

787 Save stovetop space: Cook corn on the cob in a cooler by pouring boiling water over the corn. Simmer for 5 minutes and serve. Don't leave them in for longer than 15 minutes or they will start to get tough.

788 Set out a clearly marked dirty dishes bin in a place where guests can easily see it.

789 Write your guests' meat doneness preferences on their buns with ketchup or mustard.

790 Freeze small water balloons and toss them in a cooler to keep your alcohol bottles cold.

791 Serving punch? Make an ice block to keep it cool. It melts much more slowly than ice cubes.

792 Tie a bottle opener to the handle of the drink tub or cooler.

793 Always have bug spray and sunscreen handy.

794 Use a muffin tin for a cute and original condiment tray. Plus, it makes for an easy cleanup.

795 Pre-scoop your ice cream and store it in the freezer to speed up the dessert serving process.

796 Adding two handfuls of salt to a cooler of ice water will chill drinks much faster.

797

If you suspect someone's checking you out, yawn. If they yawn back, they were. Yawning is visually contagious.

798

Want to make cheap vodka taste better? Run it through a Brita water filter pitcher.

799

Create a beer sleeve by carefully cutting off the top and bottom of a soda can. Then, cut the soda can ring in half and wrap it around your beer can. Now you can drink anywhere!

800

Flip a pizza box around on your lap so when opened the lid covers your chest. You now have made yourself a Pizza Bib!

801

Sprinkle salt on a napkin before putting a drink on it to prevent it from sticking to your cup.

802

If you ever have to clean up vomit (and hopefully you don't), put ground coffee on it first. It takes away the smell and dehydrates it. Then, you can just sweep it up.

803

Tape pool noodles to the edge of a container.
Add some ice and your favorite drinks for a
homemade floating cooler.

804

Use lollipops to stir mixed drinks and give
them extra flavor.

805

An iPhone app called BAC Alcohol Calculator
can tell you exactly how drunk you are after
entering your weight and type of beverage.

806

You can clear a room full of cigarette smoke in about a minute by spinning a wet towel around.

807

If you're ever in a fight, the best spots to hit the other person are the ones where it feels good to be massaged.

808

Want someone's number at a party? Take a picture with them and ask them to send it to you.

809

When meeting someone for the first time, ask them what they like to do rather than what they do. It'll get them excited and make for better conversation.

810

Any person who doesn't want to use protection probably hasn't used it with other partners.

811

Mix vodka and gummy candies in a container and wait a day. Then get drunk while snacking!

812

Suspect someone is giving you the wrong phone number? Read it back to them incorrectly, and if they correct you, it's legit.

813

If you're ever drunk and need to sleep in your car, take the keys out of the ignition. It's actually considered a DUI if the keys are in there while you're in the car.

814

Easiest way to sneak booze into any festival or outdoor event: Hollow out a baguette and place your favorite liquor bottle in it.

815

When filming video at a concert using your phone, put a finger over your phone's microphone. It'll sound clearer when you play it back.

816

Mountain Dew was originally invented to be mixed with whiskey. Try it!

817

Not sure if someone is interested in you? Look at their eyes. People's pupils expand by about 45% when looking at a love interest.

818

Those lines on red Solo cups are actually alcohol measurements.

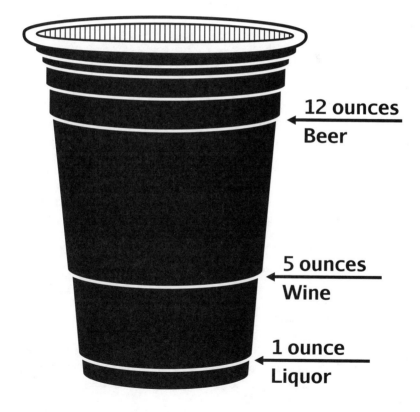

12 ounces
Beer

5 ounces
Wine

1 ounce
Liquor

10 Ways to Cure a Hangover

819 Try honey on crackers. The fructose in the honey will help flush out the alcohol in your system.

820 Believe it or not, soaking your feet in hot water will help your head feel better.

821 Drink sports drinks. They always have excellent hydrating agents in them.

822 Eat a big, greasy meal before you start drinking. Grease lines your stomach and prepares it for the night's battle.

823 Drink one glass of water for every alcoholic drink you have and you'll get drunk without getting a hangover.

824 Eat some toast. Toast will bring your blood sugar levels back up to normal after a hard night on your liver.

825 Drink lighter beer. The darker the color of the alcohol you're drinking, the worse your hangover will be.

826 Go for a walk, run, or swim. Although it may not be fun at first, it will release endorphins and improve your mood.

827 Drink water with an Alka-Seltzer. They even have a Morning Relief formulation specifically designed for hangovers.

828 Drink Pedialyte, a children's medicine. It's designed to replenish and rehydrate your body with electrolytes and has been known to work wonders. It also comes in an ice pop form if you want a cure and a treat.

829

Always buy the first pitcher or round of drinks. You'd be surprised how long you can drink on the phrase "I bought the first one."

830

If you know you're going to vomit, eat some vanilla ice cream first. It won't stop the vomiting, but it will stop the burning sensation.

831

When throwing a punch, clench your fist only at the last second. You lose a lot of power clenching throughout the swing.

832

Cheap party speaker: If you want to amplify the sound from your smartphone when you're listening to music, put it in a plastic Solo cup.

833

If you're the designated driver, tell the bartender. Oftentimes, they'll give you soda and/or food for free!

834

Look at someone's elbow when you high-five. You'll never miss again.

835

Never take ibuprofen on an empty stomach to cure a hangover. It can actually tear your stomach lining.

836

At a party and forgot to bring alcohol? Tell people you're not drinking. Everyone will suddenly offer you a free drink!

837

If you're drunk and have the urge to vomit, taking short, rapid breaths can help it go away.

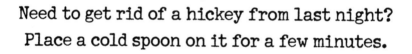

Need to get rid of a hickey from last night? Place a cold spoon on it for a few minutes.

839

When out with friends, place your phones stacked face-down in the middle of the table. First one to check their phone pays the bill!

840

If you can't afford a cab ride home, you definitely can't afford a DUI.

841

Make flower-shaped ice by filling the bottom of any two-liter soda bottle with water and the food coloring of your choice. Freeze the bottle for a few hours and then cut it open to reveal the shaped ice.

842

Hide your beer in a soft drink cup. Keep ice at the bottom to keep it cool and put the straw through the top. No one will ever know the difference!

843

Mix cotton candy with champagne or spice-infused vodka for a great party drink.

844

A wineglass in a bowl makes for a great chips 'n' dip set.

845

Run out of places to keep drinks cold at a party? Put some ice in the washing machine and use it as an extra cooler.

846

Buy your alcohol at Costco or Sam's Club. You don't need a membership and it's usually 25-35% off. It's great for when you're hosting a party, but keep in mind that you may have to do a little persuading with the card checker employee if they're unaware of this policy.

CHAPTER 9

Around the House

847

The best way to clean a microwave: Put a cup of hot water and vinegar inside, turn it on for three to five minutes, and wipe clean with ease.

848

Use a blow dryer to instantly defog any mirror.

849

Get a small pan and fill it with water. Add some vanilla extract and cinnamon and put it on the stove. Your house will smell like a delicious bakery in no time.

850

When washing windows, squeegee vertically outside and horizontally inside. That way if you see streaks, you'll know which side they're on.

851

Out of toilet cleaner? Use lemon-flavored Kool-Aid mix. The citric acid helps remove stains and the lemon flavor leaves your bathroom smelling great. Just sprinkle in a pack, swirl it around with a toilet brush, and let it sit for a few hours.

852

Spiders hate peppermint oil. Put some in a squirt bottle with water, spray your garage and door frames, and watch the spiders run!

853

Sick of having a box of tangled cords? Use old toilet paper rolls to organize them.

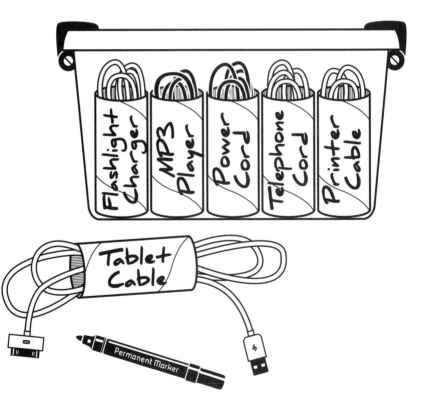

854

No dryer sheets? Throw in two tinfoil balls for static-free clothes every time.

855

Put a bar of unopened soap in your clothing drawers. It'll make them smell extra fresh.

856

When putting together build-it-yourself furniture, use a muffin tin or ice cube tray to separate all the screws, nails, and fasteners. This will make for easy access during the build.

857

Can't catch a fly? Spray it with Windex. This will immobilize it and make for an easy kill.

858

In a rush to dry your clothes? Throw a dry bath towel into the dryer along with your wet clothes. They'll dry much faster.

859

Take a picture of your fridge and pantry on your phone before you go grocery shopping. You'll never forget anything at the store again!

860

Keep a laundry basket in the back of your car to carry lots of groceries in easily.

861

Don't have a sprinkler? Just poke some holes in a two-liter soda bottle and attach it to the end of a hose.

10 Unusual Uses for Tennis Balls

862   Boots or heels leave a scuff mark on your floor? Rub a tennis ball over the mark and it'll come right out.

863   Run out of dryer sheets? Toss a few tennis balls in for a suitable replacement.

864   Keep your rainy day cash safe. Cut open a slit in a tennis ball, stuff in some money, and store it in a safe place. No burglar will ever steal a tennis ball!

865   Get rid of nasty goop and human oils from your pool by throwing in a tennis ball.

866   Protect your floors by putting one tennis ball on each of the four legs of a chair.

867   Back acting up? Lie on a tennis ball for a great DIY back massage.

868   Childproof those sharp table corners with a tennis ball that's been cut open halfway.

869   Wrap a tennis ball in sandpaper for an easy grip while sanding things.

870   Stick a tennis ball onto a tripod mount on the bottom of your camera for a soft on-the-go camera mount.

871   Hang a tennis ball from a piece of string in your garage so you know where to stop when parking your car.

The best way to fold a T-shirt: Fold the bottom fourth of your shirt up. Place the left side of the shirt toward the center, folding at the shoulder, and do the same with the right side. Fold the right sleeve in toward the center so that the left side is folded neatly. Fold the bottom half of the shirt up and flip the entire shirt over, so that the folds are hidden beneath.

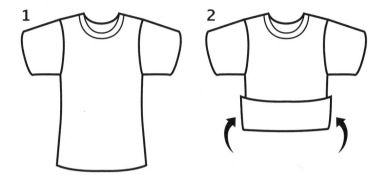

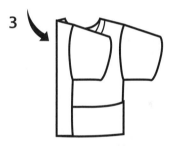

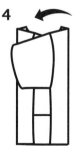

873

Put a magnet at the bottom of your hammer, so you can stick nails to it. This is a great trick for when you're on a ladder or in an awkward space.

874

Looking for something? Scan right to left with your eyes. You'll pick up more since your brain isn't used to reading that way.

875

Putting a small amount of 7UP in a flower vase will surprisingly preserve them for much longer.

876

Put a condiment cap on the top of your vacuum to easily clean out keyboards, electronics, and other small, fragile items.

877

Forget using all those gross chemicals to kill ants. Instead, just get a spray bottle, fill it three-quarters full with water and the remaining quarter with salt. Shake well and spray the colony.

878

Put dryer sheets on the back of a fan while it's blowing. They'll stick to the back of it and make a room smell amazing.

879

When drilling, fold a Post-it note to catch
the dust as it falls.

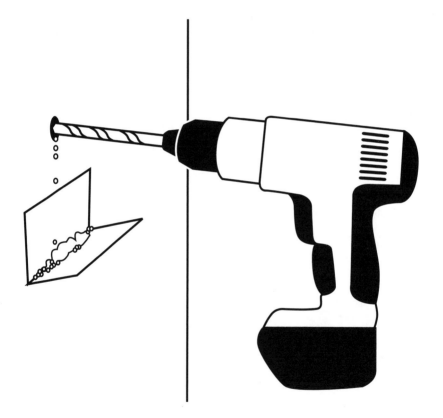

If you don't own an ironing board, throw your wrinkled clothes in the dryer with a wet sock for thirty minutes.

By adding a pinch of salt to your load of laundry you can actually brighten the colors of your clothes.

Put a used, wet sponge in the microwave for two minutes to kill 99% of the bacteria in it.

883

Need to sharpen your knives? Cut through some pieces of aluminum foil.

884

When storing empty airtight containers, throw in a pinch of salt to keep them from getting stinky.

885

Got the sniffles? Take an empty tissue box and attach it to a full tissue box with elastic bands. Put your used tissues in the empty box and throw it away when it's full.

886

Break a piece of glass? Put bread on it. The consistency of the bread will pick up even the smallest of shards.

887

If you want a streak-free shine on windows, use newspaper.

888

Dip the top of your keys in different-colored paint so you can easily tell them apart.

889

Clothes shrink too small? Soak them in a mixture of hot water and hair conditioner for five minutes and then air-dry them.

890

LED light bulbs will attract a lot fewer bugs than non-LED light bulbs.

891

Did you know pots come with a built-in spoon holder? The slot at the end of the handle is perfect for holding on to spoons when you're not stirring the pot.

892

Hate that dust in the last couple bowls of cereal? Pour it into a strainer first. Problem solved!

893

Febreze kills ants on contact and doesn't leave your house smelling like poison.

894

Cut open toilet paper rolls and use them as a cuff to save your wrapping paper from unrolling.

895

Stack your clothes vertically so you can see them more easily and save time in the morning.

Out of pillowcases? Use a T-shirt.

Put old newspaper at the bottom of your trash bin. It will absorb any food juices and make for a cleaner disposal.

Sick of bathroom mirrors fogging up? Rub a little bit of soapy water on them before you hop into the shower.

899

Have flies in your house? They are attracted to bright lights. Use this knowledge to guide them out windows or your doors.

900

When moving homes, make sure the toolbox is always the last thing you pack and the first thing you take off the truck.

901

Homemade Febreze Air Freshener: Mix 2 tablespoons of baking soda, $\frac{1}{8}$ cup of fabric softener, and hot water, and pour the mixture into an empty spray bottle.

902

Put a magnet behind your light switch for a simple, yet awesome, way to hold your keys.

903

Nothing kills weeds and keeps them dead for longer than white vinegar straight from the bottle.

904

Need to iron a shirt but don't have the time? Hang it up in the bathroom as you shower. All the wrinkles will come out by the time you're done.

905

Drill a couple small holes in the lower side of a garbage can. This gets rid of any suction issues and will make putting in and taking out bags much easier.

906

Putting two hinges on one side of a painting is a perfect way to hide the thermostat while still having easy access to it.

907

Old wine racks make for a fun and unique bathroom towel holder.

908

When you're finished painting a room, put some of the same paint in a baby jar for quick touch-ups.

909

Put an extra shower rod opposite your curtain to have easy access to loofahs, sponges, soap on a rope, and anything else you might need.

910

Lining the perimeter of your garage with pool noodles can save your car from a few dings.

911

Placing multiple ice cubes on your carpet can remove those annoying indentations left by tables, chairs, and other pieces of furniture.

912

The best way to remove pet hair from your carpet is to use a squeegee.

913

Place a rubber band over any stripped screw
to easily unscrew it.

914

Worried about all the gross bacteria on your
kid's Legos? Throw them in a mesh laundry
bag and put them through the wash.

915

Out of Swiffer pads? Old socks work almost as
well. Just make sure they're clean before you
use them.

916

Clean up water stains easily by rubbing them
with a sliced lemon.

917

Showerhead not working like it used to? Pour some white vinegar into a plastic bag and secure it to the head with a rubber band. Run the shower for a bit and it'll be good as new.

918

Food container smell bad even after you've washed it? Toss in a crunched-up piece of newspaper and leave it overnight. The smell will be gone by the morning.

919

Add a tablespoon of coarse salt while washing your pots and pans to make sure you get all the grease and grime out.

920

Never lose your remotes again! Keep them in one place by fixing double-sided squares of sticky tape to the edge of a coffee table and then stick them back there every time you're done watching TV.

921

Need a better grip on something like a jar, hammer, or screwdriver? Wrap a few rubber bands around it.

922

You can easily remove crayon marks from walls by dabbing a bit of gel-free toothpaste on them. Rub gently and then rinse it off with warm water.

923

Before hammering a nail into your wall,
place a piece of sticky tape on the spot. This
will prevent any chipping or cracking.

924

Tired of those swimming goggles always being
dirty? Make them crystal clear by smearing
a thin coat of toothpaste on the inside and
then wiping it off.

925

Lifting up on a door while opening or
closing it will often keep it from squeaking
and waking people up.

926

If a bird ever gets into your house, turn off
all of the lights and open a door or window
to the outside where there is visible light.

927

Believe it or not, rubbing a walnut on
damaged wooden furniture can cover up a lot
of dings and scratches.

928

If your toothpaste says it repairs teeth,
make sure it contains "NovaMin" as an active
ingredient. It's the only ingredient that
actually does repair teeth.

CHAPTER 10

School

929

Chew gum when you're studying, and then
chew the same flavor when you take the test.
This has been known to improve memory.

930

Trying to get a summer job? Put that you
were *Time*'s 2006 person of the year on your
resume. In 2006, *Time* made "Everyone" the
person of the year.

931

You're 50% more likely to remember
something if you speak it out loud instead of
simply reading it over and over.

932

Stumped on a project or presentation? Try ditching the computer and writing by hand. The experience has been proven to help creativity.

933

Replace the "en" in a Wikipedia link with "simple" to strip away the complex and mostly irrelevant information on the page.

934

Dorm room a little stinky? Put dry tea bags around your room. They will absorb the unpleasant odor.

935

Mathway.com solves all kinds of math homework problems with step-by-step explanations.

936

When doing a presentation in PowerPoint, always save it as a "PowerPoint Show" (.ppsx). This will open it directly to the slideshow.

937

Writing an essay? Copy and paste it into Google translate and have the computer read it out to you. It'll be much easier to find errors this way.

938

Need to read faster? Place a piece of your favorite candy on each paragraph. When you reach each paragraph you get to eat that piece.

939

If your calculator runs out of batteries in the middle of an exam, rub the ends of the batteries together. This can give you up to an extra fifteen minutes of battery life.

940

If you're giving a big presentation, have a friend ask you a set question. This way, you can come up with a great answer beforehand and it will look like you really know your stuff.

941

Study your notes within one day of taking them. Retention rates are 60% higher then.

942

Paper due? Low on black ink? Change the font color to dark tan. It looks almost identical to black ink.

943

Take notes on your professors' political ideologies and use this to your advantage when writing essays.

944

Keep pen thieves away: Put a blue ink
cartridge in a red pen. No one steals red pens.

945

You can remember the value of pi (3.1415926)
by counting each word's letters in "May I
have a large container of coffee."

946

Changing the font size of periods from 12 to
14 can make a paper look significantly longer.

947

Taking a quick nap after learning something
new can solidify that memory in your brain.

10 Ways to Increase
Your Brain Power

948 Memorize something. Train your brain to recall numbers, names, and dates.

949 Experience something new. Do something outside your comfort zone and step away from your daily routine once in a while.

950 Play Tetris. Playing Tetris can increase brainpower by almost 150%.

951 Get off the couch. Exercise and make sure you're getting your heart rate up every single day.

952 Think positively. Positivity, especially in the future tense, speeds up the creation of cells and reduces stress and anxiety, which actually kill brain neurons.

953 Eat healthy. Most people know this, but most still don't do it.

954 Read a book.

955 Get the right amount of sleep.

956 Turn off your GPS and use street signs and a map to navigate.

957 Stop using a calculator and put your brain to work.

958

If you're up late doing homework, listen
to Hans Zimmer Pandora. His music has
no distracting lyrics and the scores are
intended to motivate you.

959

At Chegg.com, you can rent expensive
textbooks online for a semester instead of
buying them at a bookstore.

960

The EasyBib iPhone app will give you a
bibliography on any book if you simply scan
the barcode.

961

Stop using Google.com to search information for school essays. Use "scholar.google .com" instead. You'll find more relevant information right away.

962

Leave studying to the very last minute? Your best chance of passing is to study the first and last 20% of the syllabus.

963

Stumped on a question or math problem? Lie down. Your thought process is much faster when you're lying down, which is why you always lie down at psychiatrist appointments.

964

Didn't finish your paper? Copy and paste a bunch of random symbols in a Word document and hand it in. Your teacher will think the file was damaged, buying you more time to finish.

965

Want to find a good job after college? Make friends with as many people in your field that are on track to graduate one or two years ahead of you.

966

One of the best ways to study is to pretend that you're going to have to teach the material.

Never send your resume to someone as a Word document (unless asked). Send it as a .PDF file since it's much cleaner and more professional looking.

Playing with puppies and kittens relieves stress and can help students perform better on exams.

969

Have a separate user account on your laptop for presentations. This way, embarrassing personal things won't show up when you open it up in class.

970

SelfControl is a program that blocks sites like Facebook, Twitter, and e-mail for a specified period of time. Using it will help you minimize distractions while you study or do homework.

971

When proofreading, read the document out loud to yourself. Your mouth will catch errors your mind might glance over.

972

You can get most answers to math assignments online by typing in the name of the textbook and then "answers."

973

Being surrounded by the color yellow will help you stay focused. Yellow decreases the production of melatonin, the hormone that makes you sleepy.

974

You are more likely to remember something you've written in blue ink than something you've written in black ink.

975

When doing long assignments, set a thirty-minute timer and race it. This will prevent you from procrastination.

976

If a website is blocked on your school's Internet, you can use Google Translate as a proxy. Just copy and paste the URL into it.

977

There is a free website called EssayTyper that lets you type a topic and will write the paper for you in minutes. Always use this website with caution.

978

Want to remember your notes more easily? Use a weird font style. Studies have shown the uniqueness of a font will make you more likely to remember what's written.

979

Need some good music to do homework to?
Try video game or movie soundtracks.
They're designed specifically to provide
backgrounds that won't mess with your
concentration.

980

It's actually better to take exams on an empty
stomach. Hunger makes you focus better.

981

Want to write essays and bibliographies like
a pro? Get the information from Wikipedia
and cite the sources listed at the bottom.

982

Need to improve your geography quickly? Buy a world map shower curtain. You'll become an expert in no time!

983

Eating chocolate while studying helps the brain retain new information more easily, and has been directly linked to higher test scores.

984

Learning a new language? Try to find a translation of your favorite book from when you were a kid.

985

If you're pulling an all-nighter,
have a fifteen- to twenty-minute nap just
before the sun comes up and your body will
reset itself.

986

Get a study partner with blue eyes. Studies
show that blue-eyed individuals study
more effectively and tend to perform
better on exams.

987

When you graduate college or university,
make sure to hold on to your college ID.
You'll usually still be able to get student
discounts because most places only look at
the photo, not the graduation year.

10 Foods That
Will Make You Smarter

988 Avocados

989 Blueberries

990 Assorted nuts

991 Oatmeal

992 Pomegranate

993 Chocolate

994 Tuna

995 Eggs

996 Tomatoes

997 Beans

998

Don't skip on sleep. Sleep is more important than homework: It's proven that it's better to get a good sleep than to stay up late cramming for exams.

Minor in what you love and major in what
will get you a job.

1000

If you're having trouble with a math problem,
plug the equation into WolframAlpha.com and
it will solve it for you.

Index